PRAISE FOR **THE FUNDAMENTALS**

"*The Fundamentals* gets to the point quickly and succinctly. It should be read by men and women who have forgotten their dreams; by those who have achieved, but have not found fulfillment; and by young people frustrated or lost in their hopes and plans. And it should be read a second time by all."
—Peter Vescey

"Isiah Thomas is one of the most fundamentally sound players who has ever played the game of basketball. This, along with a tremendous attention to detail, have been carryovers into all that he has done in the business world."
—Bob Knight, Men's Basketball Coach,
Texas Tech University

"Isiah Thomas is among the most intriguing people I've encountered in sports. An independent thinker whose mind is as quick as was his first step on the court, he has always had broad interests and ambitions, and has boldly pursued them. In this book he shows many of the insights he's developed along the way."
—Bob Costas, NBC Sports

"*The Fundamentals* was written by an individual who has won at every level in different capacities. A great player and better leader. Read and learn."
—Chuck Daly, Championship Coach

"Isiah's philosophy and commitment to the principle of extracting ideas from the entire team and working together helped us achieve our mutual goals and built a foundation of respect and friendship. . . . *The Fundamentals* perfectly illustrates Isiah's winning strategies. Don't bet against the Pacers in the next few years."

—**Kevin Wulff, Vice President, Nike, Inc.**

"This is more than a book on how to be successful. It's a book on how to navigate life and end up a winner, no matter where you start the journey. The stories of Isiah's upbringing on Chicago's West Side are riveting, and his tales of winning NCAA and NBA championships are extremely entertaining. Isiah effectively weaves the fundamentals that have made him successful throughout the story of his fascinating life."

—**Dick Ebersol, Chairman, NBC Sports and Olympics**

"If you want to better understand the facts of life—and success—you've found the right book! Isiah is a true mentor and motivator in every aspect."

—**Reggie Miller, All-Star Guard**

"Isiah Thomas shares the secrets that have made him a winner on and off the court in *The Fundamentals*. This book offers an inspirational, easy-to-read formula for success in the business of life. Isiah's entertaining personal examples, told in a down-to-earth, straight-to-the-point manner, make his lessons for setting and reaching his goals hard to miss."

—**Dennis Archer, Mayor of Detroit**

THE FUNDAMENTALS

THE
FUNDAMENTALS

8 PLAYS FOR WINNING THE GAMES OF BUSINESS AND LIFE

ISIAH THOMAS

HarperBusiness
An Imprint of HarperCollins*Publishers*

HarperCollins books may be purchased for educational, business, or sales promotional use. For information please write: Special Markets Department, HarperCollins Publishers Inc., 10 East 53rd Street, New York, NY 10022.

FIRST EDITION

Designed by William Ruoto

Library of Congress Cataloging-in-Publication Data

Thomas, Isiah, 1961–
    The fundamentals: 8 Plays for Winning the Games of Business and Life / by
Isiah Thomas—1st ed.
      p. cm.
    ISBN 0-06-662074-0 (alk. paper)
    1. Success—Psychological aspects. I. Title.

BF637.S8 T5223 2001
158—dc21
                                         2001016748

01 02 03 04 05 ❖/QW 10 9 8 7 6 5 4 3 2

The lessons in this book came from Mary Thomas, my mother and role model whose own life exemplifies determination and perseverance. I owe her everything.

As Gladys Knight sang, "If anyone should ever write my life story. . . ." The best thing that has ever happened to me is my family: my wife, Lynn, and our children, Josh and Lauren. This book, and all that I do, is dedicated to them.

ACKNOWLEDGMENTS

I had a great team for this book. Writer and ever-aspiring point guard Wes Smith was the assist leader in helping me put together the proposal and the book itself. He stayed with me during an incredibly hectic period in which I bought the CBA, took the Indiana Pacers head coaching job, and moved through our first season. He also interviewed many members of my support team including my mother, my sister Ruby, my brother Lord Henry, and several of my closest friends including Gene Pingatore, Charles Grantham, Tony Brown, Father Ted Sanchez, and Ted and Sue Kalinowski. I thank them all for their help with this project. Thanks also to my agents Jordan Bazant and Jan Miller, and my editor Mauro DiPreta at HarperCollins.

CONTENTS

THE FUNDAMENTALS

INTRODUCTION

Not long ago I was flying into Chicago and as the leased jet descended over my old hometown, my life suddenly came into sharp focus. From 20,000 feet, I could see the weary bones of my boyhood neighborhood on the West Side, and with just a slight turn of my head to the east, I could see the glittering downtown area where I was headed for a business meeting: the Loop. The Miracle Mile. The Gold Coast. The Lakefront and Navy Pier. They were all right there together, yet those celebrated parts of the city seemed so out of reach when I was growing up that they might as well have been a million miles away.

My mother, two sisters, six brothers, and I were a true ghetto family. We fought and scraped—and occasionally begged—for every bit of food, every piece of clothing. We must have lived in every corner of the West Side at one time or another, on the run from one landlord, one bill collector, or another. Most of Chicago did not seem open to me then. I looked to it as the Emerald City, a forbidden zone reserved for people of another color and social class. I watched them flash through my neighborhood on trains and along the Eisenhower Expressway each morning while my brothers and I did the reverse commute. We hustled for our daily fare in the toughest wards of the inner city and blue-collar suburbs. We shined shoes for a quarter a pair on street corners and in dark taverns. Then we fought our way home, trying to hang on to enough coins for a meal.

You might find it difficult to believe, but I didn't really see the Chicago that most people know until I was nineteen years old and on the "visiting team." I was a rookie with the Detroit Pistons of the NBA (National Basketball Association) and we'd come to play the Chicago Bulls. My new teammates expected me to show them around the city but they didn't want to go to the parts of it that I could take them to. In truth, I was as much a visitor to Chicago's affluent core as any of my teammates, any tourists, or conventioneers.

THE VIEW FROM BOTH SIDES

Since then, I've seen both sides of my hometown, and both sides of the world too. Looking out the jet's window, I reflected on how far I'd traveled at that point in my journey from boyhood to manhood. I'd gone from the hard life of a dirt-poor ghetto kid to the glory and rewards of winning national basketball championships at both the college and professional levels, and being inducted into the NBA Hall of Fame. I've also had considerable entrepreneurial success as the owner and co-owner of businesses that included the nation's third largest printing franchise. Most recently, I've enjoyed my first season as the head coach of the Indiana Pacers NBA team. I had never planned to become a coach, but after I'd been out of the game a while I realized how much I missed being intimately involved in it. I wanted to be successful in other arenas because my family had always emphasized that you should do more with your mind and energies than participate in sports. But the more time I spent in business meetings, the more I realized that I hadn't just loved playing the sport, I'd really enjoyed all of the competitive aspects, from plotting game strategies to bringing together a group of individuals and building a team.

My life has been a study in contrasts. I've known defeat and despair, and I've had many incredible victories. I've lived in stunting poverty and I've been blessed with lucrative opportunities. I've trembled in dark corners with a gun to my head, and I've stood in the spotlight of thundering arenas basking in the cheers of thousands of fans. I've felt the deadening forces of the ghetto and I've experienced the awesome power of dreams realized in full. I could see it all from my seat in the jet above Chicago that day: Where I'd been. Where I was going. And what had helped me get this far.

Reflecting on my life that day and since then, it's struck me that I've benefited tremendously from the wisdom, guidance, and assistance of others. From family members to teachers, coaches, teammates, and business leaders, I've had many people reach out to me to share their knowledge. Maybe it's because I was the youngest in my family, but I've always seen myself as a student. I was always looking to my parents and my older brothers and sisters for advice. Whenever I've faced a challenge in my personal life or in my career, I've looked for sources of wisdom and experience. Now, it is my turn to share what I have learned from my guides and teachers and from my own experiences.

I was inspired to write this book by the young people who seek me out wherever I go. A lot of them come to me for advice on basketball, of course, but many who know my background of poverty are also moved to ask me how I made it when so many others don't. They are searching for guidance, just as I did. Some may be more qualified to give them advice, but there aren't many who relate to their struggles as closely as I do.

The successes I've had aren't due to any great athletic gifts I was born with. Believe me, I could name at least a couple dozen guys from the old neighborhood—my own brothers among them—who were better natural athletes than I could ever hope to be. There are plenty who were bigger, stronger, faster, and more agile. I made it because I was willing to accept the help that was so generously offered to me, and because I realized early on that there were certain things that were fundamentally important to achieving success. I didn't sit down one day as a boy and identify those fundamentals. They came to me over the course of many years. They are the themes that appear again and again in my life. Without my realizing it, they became the guidelines by which I lived as a young man and even now, at the ripe old age of thirty-nine.

When I reached the point where other people looked to me for guidance, I found myself talking about those fundamentals in private conversations and in my speeches. This book is my way of sharing them with a larger audience so that others might benefit from what I've learned. I'll be telling you a lot about the environment that I grew up in, in part because I want you to understand that I started out with nothing other than a family that cared deeply about each other. I made it with their help and the determination that they taught me. My hope is that you will see that if I made it, you can too. The key things that have helped me along the way include:

- My dreams about the possibilities for a better life
- My goals at each stage of life
- The lessons I've learned from mentors and role models
- My experiences as a leader on teams and within organizations
- My inner sources of strength and commitment
- The values I've learned and lived by
- My determination to seek and capitalize on opportunities
- The great rewards I've reaped and shared with others

Most people who pick up a book like this want to move their lives forward, and so they are already on the right track. They are seeking information and knowledge rather than an easy way out. Too often, people try to escape their circumstances rather than rising above them. Too often, they try to dull their pain rather than sharpen their minds. They let what has happened to them destroy them, rather than daring to dream of better things and then pursuing them.

I doubt that I would have had the successes I've had in life if it weren't for the survival lessons I learned on the West Side. I'm a big believer in the saying: "That which does not destroy us makes us stronger." I have many painful memories of people close to me who were destroyed by poverty and despair. There is rarely a day that passes without a visit from one of those memories. I try to use them to drive myself rather than letting them drag me down. I prefer to think of my past as a source of inner strength, and I would advise you to do the same. When I go back to my old neighborhood, whether in my mind or in person, even my worst experiences are sources of strength and inspiration. I came from nothing and I've built a great life, so I have no fear of losing everything. That self-confidence is liberating, and it is something I'd like to pass on to you.

As I flew into Chicago en route to a business meeting that day, I looked to the West Side to see if I could spot my old home court at Gladys Playground. I was surprised that I couldn't see it right away. I figured "the Hole" would be visible from at least 50,000 feet up, if not from the moon. Geographically, Gladys Playground is at the corner of South Spaulding and West Gladys near Garfield Park on the West Side. Personally, it was at the center of my life growing up.

I have to be careful how I talk about Gladys, because someone may overhear me and think I've got a girlfriend. Gladys, you see, was very important to me. I love her and think of her often, even if she was the playground-equivalent of a bag lady. Gladys was a ghetto playground with all of the standard ghetto amenities. Broken glass. Dry drinking fountains. Steel bars across the restroom doors. Hot and cold running gang fights. Its basketball court had more pits, cracks, and craters than the old parquet floor at Boston Gardens. Weeds and gravel claimed equal shares of what was not worn down to bare dirt. And then, there was the Hole, a man-eating abyss that gaped directly beneath one of the baskets. The Hole swallowed up balls, players, entire teams. You had to watch out for the Hole when you went to the bucket at Gladys Park. It was responsible for an orthopedic casualty list of blown-out knees and backs. Legend had it that some of the best street players ever to live on the West Side went in there with big dreams and came out as just more guys with "cudda-been" stories.

Like most ghetto courts, the hoops at Gladys Playground wore no nets. Some guys brought their own, but if they lost or quit, the nets went home with them. They would leave the other guys begging, "Oh man, don't take the net. . . ." but you didn't just leave your net. It wouldn't last through the night. My boyhood home court was a unique place in other ways. One rim was a few inches lower than the other, and the high rim was bent to the left side. When the wind was blowing, you might as well forget about shooting from the outside. Come to think of it, playing at Gladys was a lot like playing at the old Boston Gardens. No disrespect to Larry Bird and the Celtics, but it was tougher to win on Gladys, where the winners stayed and losers walked. If you lost, you might not get back on the court for a week. They didn't take reservations. You had to call next game and be there when your turn came up.

It was a big hangout, and safer than most places in a ten-block radius. During the day at least, you could be pretty sure that nobody was going to try and rob you or shoot you on the court. When you stepped off, though, you were back on uncertain turf. I got caught one time walking home from Gladys. I was probably twelve or thirteen. I'd been playing after school. It was around six o'clock. Two guys snatched me up. They dragged me into an alleyway between two buildings and put a gun to my head.

The poor robbing the poor.

"How much money you got, Shortie?"

I didn't have any money. I never had any money. One of them jammed his sandpaper hand up into my neck and started choking me. Meanwhile, the other gangster tried to push the gun barrel through my skull. They worked well together. Both jammed their free hands into my pants pockets and rifled through them. Their stinking breath gagged me. Coming up empty, one of them bent in front of my face and for the first time looked into my eyes. Something flashed. He jerked up and stepped back like a guy who just realized he was robbing the wrong bank.

"Are you Mama Thom's son?"

"Yeah."

"Rat's brother?"

"Yeah."

"Go on, get the hell out of here!"

I scrambled out of the alleyway, wiped the tears out of my eyes, and sprinted for home. Saved by family ties once again.

MY DEAR, GHETTO SUPERSTAR

My mother, Mary, who is known as "Dear" to all of her children and closest friends because of the love and respect we have for her, and as "Mama Thom" to most everyone else on the West

Side, ran the youth center at Our Lady of Sorrows Catholic Church for many years. It was not a prestigious, high-profile Chicago job like alderman, ward boss, or bag man, but in our neighborhood it came with clout. The youth center was one of the few places where kids could hang out and not get hung out. It was the Switzerland of the inner city. Neutral territory. A safe haven. And my mother controlled who got in the door. She also had the power to kick anybody out. It paid to be nice to Mama Thom but my mother built up a lot of good will on her own. My oldest brother, Lord Henry (nicknamed "Rat"), says she raised a whole neighborhood, and that's close to the truth. The only things she had to give were her time, her compassion, her labors, and her courage, and she gave all of that in abundance.

Dear was a true ghetto superstar. She had the ultimate power. She feared nothing. She wasn't afraid to help you, or hurt you if you threatened anyone she cared for. She befriended priests, nuns, gang bangers, hookers, pimps, cops, and cons. Because of her—and my brothers too—I got a pass from most, but not all, of the predators on the West Side. They'll tell you I was the spoiled child in the family because I was the last of the brood. I suppose that's true from their perspective. But being spoiled in my neighborhood wasn't like being spoiled in Scarsdale, Beverly Hills, or Lake Forest. Being spoiled in the Thomas family meant that you got one whole piece of chicken for dinner, and that was a feast.

SURVIVING AND THRIVING

Today, whenever someone tells me they grew up on Chicago's West Side, I can't help but shake the person's hand and say,

"Congratulations, you made it!" I have enormous respect for any person who survived an upbringing there, because I know what it takes to overcome that environment. I know also that very few make it. I was one of the lucky ones, thanks to Dear, my brothers and sisters, and Gladys, of course. Playing hoops was my salvation from the ghetto life. The basketball court was the one place where I could go and forget the hunger pangs, the robberies and beatings, and the minute-by-minute threat of violence. That's why the sport is anything but a game to me. It was my tool for getting a great education, security for my family, and entrée to the Emerald Cities that had once seemed all but closed to me and to people who looked like me.

Not that I didn't have fun playing basketball and growing up in the Thomas Gang. Even as a professional, I often wept out of sheer joy at being caught up in the flow of a great game. It still is the one place where I feel totally free. Basketball is an essential part of my spirit. I'll take a ball onto the hardwood floor even now when I need to think, to reflect, or to quiet some anger. I love basketball like others love the ocean or the mountains. But it does not define me. I stopped playing professionally when I could no longer give it my all, when my mind became distracted, when my body could no longer take me where my instincts said I should go. Then I moved on to build a life as a business entrepreneur and network sports analyst. My ventures have included an Internet shopping and gift-certificate company, a national chain of more than 400 printing centers with annual sales of nearly $200 million, a commodity brokerage, a real-estate management company, an event entertainment company, and a nonprofit foundation that benefits people who are where I once was, and where a part of me will always be.

DON'T RENT, OWN

In July of 1999, I signed a deal that put me in an entirely new neighborhood. For $10 million, I bought controlling ownership of all nine teams that then comprised the CBA. My goal was to consolidate and rejuvenate the CBA by expanding the number of franchises to twenty-two teams, and then to create a true developmental league for the NBA. I planned to pair each professional team with a CBA affiliate, just as each major-league baseball team has its own farm club. And I was going to take the CBA into cyberspace. This was the first pro league to have a live Webcast of a game! Don't let anyone tell you differently, the CBA was there first.

My ultimate aim is still to own an NBA franchise someday, but with the cost of teams now running into the hundreds of millions of dollars, I figured I had to start in the minor leagues and work my way up. It was a challenging and ultimately disappointing undertaking, but purchasing the CBA was more than a personal achievement. When I took ownership, the CBA became the only entity in professional sports to be 100 percent controlled by a minority owner. It is extremely important for African-Americans to have *ownership,* to share equally in the American dream. Black kids grow up hearing their parents talking about the day when they no longer have to pay rent or work for someone else. *Be an owner, not a renter!* It is part of what drives me, and so many others too.

Blacks have been the backbone of most sports franchises for decades now. Yet it seems like forever that we've been fighting to establish ourselves as coaches, managers, vice presidents, and owners; just as it seems like such a long time that we've been fighting for a decent share of the wealth in a nation that we've helped make strong. You may not believe it, or it may sound corny to you, but I bought the CBA for all of us. I purchased the CBA for my wife and children, my mother and sisters and brothers, the people I grew up with who never made it out of the West Side, and for all the black folks who dream of better things for themselves and their children and grandchildren. African-Americans who achieve success are expected to think beyond ourselves. I accept that. I welcome it. Shortly after I purchased the CBA, the offers started coming in from people who thought they could buy it from me by letting me make a quick profit, selling out, and moving on to the next big thing. I've got to tell you, there's a part of me that whispered, *Take the money and run. Do the business deal because the deal is the deal. Don't let your social or racial conscience enter into the game.*

But then I look into my young son's eyes and I wonder, *Why am I in this business in the first place? To make as much money as I can? Or to make greater opportunities available to people like me? What is more valuable for more people over the long run?* The business I chose is the opportunity-making business. I wouldn't be here if someone hadn't provided opportunities for me. I couldn't have gone to an integrated high school or state university if someone hadn't opened the door of opportunity for me. As the next black man through the door, my responsibility is to keep it open by hanging in there. Not selling out but building up. My mother fought to make the world a little better for me. So did Martin Luther King Jr. and Andrew Young. They kept the door open even though they knew that they wouldn't benefit nearly as much as those who would come through later.

I want to do my part because there has to be somebody up in heaven smiling down at a thirty-nine-year-old son of the ghetto who can write a check for $5 million as a down payment for his own basketball league. It was a wonderful moment for me. Then another opportunity knocked. When Larry Bird stepped in as coach of the Indiana Pacers and had considerable success, other NBA owners took notice. While other former NBA players had been successful, Bird was a superstar. His coaching success opened the gates. Suddenly, I was getting a lot of calls inquiring whether I would be interested in coaching. I couldn't lie. I was.

I'd grown to miss being directly involved in the ebb and flow of the game that I have loved since I was old enough to pick up a ball. I'm a competitive person, and being a coach is the next best thing to being on the floor as a player. The greatest gift I have is basketball. We should strive to always make the most of our gifts. Those who find something they love and then build their lives around it seem to be the happiest, most secure and fulfilled people I know. Whenever I get too far away from the game of basketball, I find myself losing focus. Looking back on my life, basketball was always the place where I could express my creativity, burn up my energy, and find joy and a sense of belonging. So, I allowed my name to be put in the hat, and eventually, the Indiana Pacers pulled it out.

Unfortunately, this wonderful opportunity had an adverse effect on my CBA plans. When the Indiana Pacers asked me to be their head coach, NBA officials said I could not own the CBA while coaching in their league. They forced me to put the CBA into a blind trust until a buyer could be found. I was not allowed to participate in its management after that. When no deal to sell the nine teams could be put together, the CBA went under.

Still, I consider myself a fortunate man. If you don't understand why I am a little stunned over the way my life has progressed, then you haven't ever been to the corner of Spaulding and Gladys in Chicago. Being Mama Thom's son, and having a bunch of older brothers who were respected and sometimes feared, helped me survive that environment. I benefited from the mistakes my brothers and their friends made. I was there when they got into drugs for the high, and I saw what happened when the high ended. What I didn't see on my own, they pointed out and made sure I understood.

I've had a whole crew of strong mentors in my life, including my high school, college, and professional coaches, assorted nuns, priests, teachers, teammates, and friends. You'll be reading about many of them in this book. None of them are saints. One or two of them have had their flaws picked over so much in the press that I'm surprised there is anything left of them. They are good, imperfect people who've brought a lot into this world. I owe them more than I can ever repay them, so I'm trying to spread my payments around by sharing what they've taught me, and a few things I've had to learn the hard way on my own.

FUNDAMENTAL LESSONS

I call these lessons "the Fundamentals," which is a term borrowed from sports, though this is not at all a book simply about games. It's intended to be a book about life. The fundamentals of basketball include the basic skills you need to be a player: shooting, passing, dribbling, rebounding, playing defense, setting picks, blocking out, and so on. Beyond the basics, there are other fundamentals that have more to do with your inner game. Those include your competitive drive, your court awareness, your willingness to play as a team member, your ability to control your emotions and channel them productively during a game. I thought I had all of the fundamentals down in grade school. Then I went to St. Joseph's High School and played for Coach Gene Pingatore, who wasted no time in letting me know that I didn't know squat about fundamental *team* basketball. By the time I graduated from St. Joseph's, which had a record of 57–5 during my junior and senior years, I was certain that I had those fundamentals down.

My new coach, Bobby Knight at Indiana University, did his best to set me straight—and in very colorful language too! I thought I picked up on Knight's version of the fundamentals pretty well. We won the NCAA championship in my sophomore year. But then I turned pro and was drafted by the Detroit Pistons. My education in basketball fundamentals, I discovered, had only just begun. I've found that it works the same way in life. Just when you think you've got it figured out, along comes another lesson in humility. I've finally begun to understand that the smartest people are those who realize how much they have to learn. I don't know it all. In one way or another, I'm still getting taken to school every day. So I offer you the following fundamentals not as some all-knowing, all-seeing wise guy but as someone who's been around a little, experienced a lot, and is still trying to figure it all out.

I may be the luckiest guy on the planet. You won't get an argument from me on that. But I've paid attention to a lot of very smart people and to the lessons that have come my way. That's what I want to share with you. The fundamentals that I've identified so far are the things that have gotten me where I am, and that keep me going even today. If you are just starting out in school, in business, in a marriage or with a family, you will find these fundamentals valuable. If you've been around a while, you may find them helpful as reminders. I've found that it never hurts to go back and check in with the people or the guidelines that have worked for you in the past.

In the first half of the 1980s, the Detroit Pistons were fighting for respectability after a long, long history of mediocrity in spite of having had some great players over the years. When Coach Chuck Daly was hired in 1983 things began to improve dramatically. We started to come together, but over the next few years, we still had difficulty against veteran teams, including the New York Knicks. They'd developed a great full-court press that gave us fits. We just couldn't seem to find a way to break that press consistently. We were being embarrassed by it.

Throughout my college and professional playing days, I always checked in with my high school coach, Mr. Pingatore, when I was having trouble with some aspect of my game. He is a great teacher with a deep understanding of basketball strategy. After a game in which the Knicks press put our offense in a straitjacket, I called Mr. Pingatore. He'd seen the Knicks work us over. "Why don't you guys run the 'press breaker'?" he asked.

Sometimes when we get thrown for a loop, it pays to go back to the fundamentals. Here I'd been wracking my brain trying to think of a way to handle the Knicks' trapping press, and all I really needed to do was think back to my high school days. Mr. Pingatore taught us a strategy that had always worked against that type of full-court press. Basically, it was a fast-break play built around putting the team's best ball handler in the middle so that he could attack the press before the other team was set up. Mr. Pingatore reminded me how it had worked in our phone conversation and he suggested ways we might tweak it for the professional level. I talked to Coach Daly about it the next day at practice. One of the great things about Chuck was his willingness to listen and try anything he thought would help the team. Sometimes he used our suggestions just to pacify us, but in this case, my old high school team's press breaker did the job.

Going back to the fundamentals of the game helped me even at the highest level of competition. In the chapters that follow, I'm going to offer you the most important life fundamentals I've identified so far in my own journey. I'm not going to hit you over the head with them, or even give you a pop quiz at the end of each chapter. Instead, I'm going to tell you what they are and then show you how I've benefited by applying them to my own life. It's a soft sell, and one I hope you'll enjoy and find helpful. I'm about as basic a person as you'll find. I've made a lot of mistakes, many of which I'll recount in this book so that you might learn from them. But I've managed to survive and find a path in life under some fairly hostile and difficult circumstances. Hopefully, you can build on my experiences and do even better.

Here are the fundamentals that I'll be offering you in the rest of the book.

The First Fundamental: Dreams Are Doorways

For some people, dreams are a luxury. Not for me. Dreams were literally all I had for a good part of my life. I may have become an all-star basketball player, but I was an all-world dreamer long before that. When I tell you that dreams are where life begins, I'm not giving touchy-feely advice. I'm telling it like it is. Dreams may be all you have right now, but they are the doors you walk through to a better life.

The Second Fundamental: Measure at the Root

Your dreams give you license to see beyond your circumstances to your *possibilities*. To transform those possibilities into realities, you need to set realistic but ambitious goals for your life. Those goals are the stepping stones that take you from where you've been to where you want to be. Each step must be firmly rooted in the dreams you have for your life so that as you pursue one goal, you can measure your progress so you stay on course.

The Third Fundamental: Go Deep for Commitment

When I think of all the poor, hungry, and struggling people I've known in my life, it's a toss-up as to whether I met more of them on the West Side of Chicago or in affluent settings such as Birmingham, Michigan, Hilton Head, South Carolina, or Los Angeles, California. Everyone I knew growing up was poor. But many of the most wealthy and successful people I've met since were carrying around memories of their own poverty, hunger, and struggles too. They used those memories to drive themselves out of poverty or whatever rut they fell into. When life challenged them, they went deep into their memories and emotional reservoirs and drew upon them. Often, they tapped into weaknesses and fear and built strength and determination. They went deep and it took them far.

The Fourth Fundamental: Learn from the Best

There was no Role Model Factory Outlet in my neighborhood. No Rent-to-Own Mentor Store. I had to take my heroes where I could find them, and they weren't the kind of role models featured in Disney movies or *Success* magazine. I couldn't be choosy, so I tried to learn from the best offered by each person I met. You might be surprised by what you can learn from the most unlikely role models and mentors, if you are willing to look for the best that is within them rather than focusing on their faults.

The Fifth Fundamental: Leadership from the Inside Out

The recognized "floor leader" on a basketball team is usually the player who dishes out the ball to teammates. The role of this player is not to assert control of the game; it's to get the ball to those in the best position to score. When I look at the NBA today, I see a lot of great players who are confused about what it takes to be a leader on and off the court. Leadership isn't about standing out. It's not about being a human highlight film. It's about helping your teammates, your coworkers, your family work together. That means helping them develop their talents, but more often it begins within you.

The Sixth Fundamental: Living with Values

People enjoy sports because things that are often subtle in real life are easier to see in games. That's particularly true when it comes to values. A basketball team that does not have a well-defined and shared set of values is defeated before it takes the floor. The game is over even if there is only one player who doesn't buy in, because the opponent will focus on that player and bring the whole team down. I know, because that's how I played the game. It's true with teams and with individuals. A strong set of values is vital to your success and to your survival in a competitive world. With them as a foundation, you can more easily act based on what you *believe in* rather than what is happening *to* you. Values give you the power to respond to challenges thoughtfully rather than emotionally.

The Seventh Fundamental: Opportunities Are Golden

Though the West Side of Chicago may not look like it, believe me, it's the veritable Land of Opportunity. There are more avid opportunists in that neighborhood than on Wall Street and Hollywood put together. When you grow up poor and black, you learn to value every opportunity to better your position in the world, and you develop an ability to find opportunities in the most unusual places.

The Eighth Fundamental: The Best Present

One of the most difficult yet basic fundamentals to master is the art of enjoying each moment that you are given on this planet. It's easy to do that, of course, when the birds are singing and life is going your way. It's not so easy when you are struggling. Yet even the struggle is a gift, if you are willing to see it that way. It is important to recognize and enjoy the gift of each moment, and it is equally important that you share the rewards that you receive so that they are multiplied.

So there you have them, life's fundamentals from the son of a ghetto superstar. Everybody on the West Side knew and respected my mother. I'd be happy to have that sort of standing and influence on the wider stage that's been made available to me. I have many friends who've made it out of the ghetto and poverty and built lives that are successful in every way. We can pick each other out of a crowd. We are drawn to each other because we share so much. One of the things we share is a certain amount of guilt and self-doubt. We're always asking, "Why me?" because we know the odds. Some might convince themselves that they simply deserve the rewards of life because they are better than anyone else. That's bull, but it might work for some people. There is a lot of luck involved in anyone's success. We all know so many other people who were smarter, more athletic, more determined than we imagined ourselves to be. And if we don't think about them, they'll come around and remind us. There are approximately five thousand people in Chicago who taught me how to dribble. Another three thousand are responsible for saving me from certain death at one time or another. It could all be true. This book is part of my effort to repay those who have reached out to me.

We all do our best to justify our success to others, even as we wonder ourselves, "Why me? Why not him or her?" We all experience those feelings. We're all hit from time to time with the thought that we've really had an unfair amount of good fortune in our lives. We want to spread it around, to share the wealth and the blessings we've experienced. I want to become the owner of an NBA team so I can do that. I bought the CBA to do that. I've written this book for that purpose too.

We are all here for a purpose, but, as the saying goes, from whom much is given, much is expected. I've been blessed and I'd like to offer this book as a small repayment with the potential for a long-term payout.

See you at the end of the game.

1.

DREAMS ARE DOORWAYS

I was the youngest in a poor family, which put me at the end of a long line for slim pickings. Standing ahead of me at the door to an empty refrigerator were Delores (the oldest), then Ruby, Lord Henry, Gregory, Larry, Mark, Preston, and Ronnie. In our house it was first-come, first-served—and anyone who came later was probably flat out of luck. It was that way for food, clothing, and even a place to sleep. Many a night I had to make my bed on the floor because I got home late after a game and there was no place else to lie down. It was just the way we lived and it didn't seem so much like a hardship at the time, except for the lack of food and the constant hunger.

I am not exaggerating when I tell you that I spent most of my childhood scratching around for something to eat. My earliest dreams were not—as you might imagine—fantasies of playing professional basketball: driving, passing, scoring, and winning NBA championships. My boyhood dreams were mostly about well-stocked refrigerators: huge refrigerators that were bursting at the hinges with mouth-watering roast chickens, heaping plates of spaghetti, and thick juicy steaks.

When there was nothing for dinner at our house, which was the usual case, I would actually go to bed early so I could dream about the food that wasn't on the table. No kidding. I would create ten-course meals in my mind and then drool over them in my sleep. Sometimes my dreams convinced my aching stomach that it was full and quieted the hunger pangs for a night.

Dreaming worked for me as a hungry child, and it continued to work for me as I grew older and my dreams changed. I bought into the power of dreams to ease my hunger pangs when I was a boy and I came to believe that dreams were doorways that you could walk through to find a better life. Every major accomplishment I've had began as a dream, so you won't find me being cynical about the subject of dreams and their power. Sure, dreams are kid stuff. They are adult stuff too. There have been many studies that show how answers, ideas, and inspiration come to us in dreams. Harvard psychiatrist Deirdre Barrett notes that the works of Beethoven were often the results of his dreams. Paul McCartney says that the song "Yesterday" came to him in a dream, and others from Ghandi to Marion Jones have attributed their accomplishments to the power of their dreams. Dreams are powerful catalysts for changing your life, and sometimes the world too. Consider the dreams of the Reverend Martin Luther King Jr. One of the most famous lines in his most celebrated speech wasn't "I have one heck of an idea." It was "I have a dream."

"I have a dream that one day on the red hills of Georgia the sons of former slaves and the sons of former slave owners will be able to sit down together at the table of brotherhood," Dr. King said. His dream was so powerful that it helped to change the world. You can't deny that sort of power. It's there. All you have to do is tap into it by daring to imagine a better way.

What are dreams? They are the expression of your creative imagination. They are the first step in determining what actions we will take to enhance our lives. Our dreams or imaginations trigger what we do and feel. We can train ourselves to dream of better things and then to act upon those dreams just as the best athletes consciously visualize themselves making a big play so that their bodies are prepared and programmed to do it during a game.

When I encourage you to dream, I'm giving you permission to live with hope instead of despair or discouragement. While your eyes might be able to see only what is going on around you right now, your imagination and your dreams can open your mind to the possibilities of a better life. If the youngest son of a ghetto mother—a boy who used to go from place to place in search of food nearly every day of the week—can one day coach an NBA team, it shouldn't be hard for you to dream of what incredible things you can do. Then, you can build upon those dreams.

My parents and my sisters and brothers supported me in my dreams of being good at sports and then slowly, they helped me build dreams of earning a college degree and building a life of achievement in other areas. I still dream of things I want to accomplish. Your dreams change as your life and circumstances change. I've reached a level of financial security that was well beyond my wildest wishes as a boy, but that doesn't mean I've stopped dreaming of other things. I'm living my earlier dreams of being able to help my mother and sisters and brothers escape poverty. I'm also living my dream of providing a secure and comfortable life for my own wife and children. This doesn't mean I've stopped conjuring up bigger and better scenarios for my life. Now I have visions of being able to do more for others outside of my immediate family.

Dreams create a vision for your life—not the life that you were born into, but one that you determine. Dreams give you reason to have hope. They open your eyes to better things. They give you a path to walk. I encourage you to never stop daring to dream. It frees you from the things that otherwise might hold you back. Dreams are just the first step in the process, but they are often the most important. Once you envision the life you want, you can then set realistic goals that will lead you there in the real world. Keep in mind that while you'll have many dreams that come and go over the years, there are certain over-riding dreams that always seem to guide the goals you set for yourself. For me, the Big One is that I've always dreamed of helping poor families like mine. I want to reach a level of power and influence—and wealth too—that will enable me to provide opportunities and inspiration for people who are still stuck in neighborhoods like the one I came from. I've been a dreamer all my life, but I've always wanted to be a dream fulfiller.

If you dare to dream and go after those dreams, you set off a powerful chain reaction. When other people see that you believe in your dreams, often they buy into them too. Not everyone will support you, of course, but there are people out there who have benefited from being dreamers and they are especially likely to reach out to others with big dreams. One of the best examples that comes to mind is Oprah Winfrey, who had a very difficult life as a child but never gave up on her dreams. And now she has a television show and all sorts of char-itable channels for helping other people get on track to their dreams.

When I encounter someone who is obviously dedicated and determined to better his or her life, I'm inclined to help them in any way I can, either through my own charitable foundation or through others I work with. Like Oprah, I know how hard it can be to overcome discouragement and despair, and, like her, I know the rewards of never giving up. I also will never forget that many people reached out to help me when I was still chasing my earliest dreams.

THE TOUGHER YOU HAVE IT, THE BIGGER YOU SHOULD DREAM

My daily existence is still tied to those very, very, lean years I experienced growing up on the West Side of Chicago. I'll always have memories of that hunger and the vivid dreams it stirred. I can remember being so hungry that I couldn't think straight. I'd do things and take chances and justify my actions—anything— just to fill that hunger. I don't think politicians understand what real hunger does to people. You can talk about social reform, education, all the other great needs of the underprivileged, but until you satisfy the basic hunger, the type of hunger that was part of my childhood, you can't expect people to focus. It is a hunger that could easily have destroyed my ability to hope for anything better in life. I was fortunate that it didn't. I was often so hungry I couldn't think about anything else. When you don't eat for a whole day, and then the next day comes and you still haven't eaten, the hunger takes over. It demands that you get something to eat. And when there is no money in your pocket, your choices are to beg, to steal, to rob, or to do things for money that you would not otherwise do. Fortunately, my mother kept a tight rein on me. She and my sisters and brothers kept me from doing anything seriously bad, but some of my friends who were equally destitute and hungry crossed the line and all I could say was, "I understand."

Hunger makes you think differently. All you want to do is get rid of that ache in your gut. You can't explain that type of pain to someone who has never experienced it. It makes you walk the streets looking for pennies on the ground, or a bit of cheese still stuck to a fast-food wrapper. I remember asking my mother for a dime, one dime, and seeing that it broke her heart that she didn't have it to give me. So I stopped asking her. I couldn't go to my older brothers because most of the time, they'd already asked me if I had anything to share. You get angry when you are that hungry and that poor. You get mad when you walk into a grocery store and it's packed with food that you can't have. You get angry when you turn on the television and there's a McDonald's or Burger King commercial. There is food all around you but you can't have it, and everybody who walks by you has a full belly, so you get mad at them too. I had friends who acted out that anger. They took it out on people and did things that if they weren't so hungry I know they wouldn't have done. Sometimes, I wanted to lash out too.

THE BEGGAR'S ROUTE

Mostly, though, I begged. Other kids had paper routes, I had a regular beggar's route. Everything within that route—school, church, the youth center, the Boy's Club, my friends' homes—was, directly or indirectly, a food source for me. My beggar's route would usually start in the school cafeteria, where I'd try to con the ladies in the kitchen into slipping me something before the lunch hour, or something *for* the lunch hour. If I didn't have any luck there, and sometimes even if I did, I'd move on to the Martin Luther King Boy's Club at Sacramento and Washington. I played basketball there for Coach Johnny Gage and his brother Sam. Some days they kept me alive. Johnny would look at me and say, "Damn, you are the *hungriest*-looking kid!" I'd ask him to buy me a hot dog, and he'd say, "Boy, you beg too much. You beg all the time." But either Johnny or Sam would usually come through for me. There were a lot of nights when if it weren't for them, I don't know what I would have done. I signed up for every sports team and club that was available, mostly because I'd learned there was usually a cookie or a snack to be had at the end of each game.

Sometimes I tried my friends' refrigerators, Willie Scott's or Michael Moody's, maybe Anthony Young's or Tyrone Brewer's. Mrs. Blakely was a teacher who'd let us come over to her house and eat. Then there was Greg Dortch. I knew my mooching had gotten bad when I went over to Greg's one day and found a padlock on the refrigerator. His parents told him they'd had enough of the Thomas boy's food raids.

I stood in some soup lines too. I wasn't there every day, but there were times when it got me through. I have strong feelings for the Reverend Jesse Jackson to this day because I was one of the kids he fed with his Operation Breadbasket.

A LIFELONG HUNGER

I've heard others who grew up poor say they didn't realize how hard they'd had it until they got older. That was not the case for me. Not that I was miserable; I was a happy kid most of the time. We had such a big and spirited family that we kept each other laughing. We are optimistic and upbeat by nature, but there was no doubt that we were poor by any standard.

We dealt with it every day. My mother worked, but for many years it was in exchange for our tuition to Catholic schools. Later, her wages as a counselor with the city's Urban Progress program barely covered the rent or the mortgage. For a long time she was on welfare and public aid, but she was too proud to use food stamps. She did sometimes bring home surplus food that had been donated to our parish. Once she brought us boxes and boxes of Hamburger Helper. No hamburger. Just the helper. We ate that for what seemed like years. Another time, she hooked up with a granola connection. Quaker Oats had developed a granola product and they were eager to get the word out, so they shipped out free samples to the West Side. We didn't have milk, but we had granola for breakfast, lunch, and dinner. That's when I decided that "health food" was a contradiction in terms. When the Hamburger Helper and granola ran out, we were left to our own devices for finding our next meals. There was a period of at least a year and a half in which I never bothered to go into the kitchen because I knew there was nothing there to eat. I learned to forage for food instead. Most days, my first thought upon waking was *Where am I going to get my next meal?* One of our favorite places to find food was the garbage bin behind the old Chicago Stadium. We'd wait there after basketball games, concerts, and other events and beg the cleanup crews to give us the unsold popcorn before they threw it away. Sometimes we'd get there too late, so we'd have to dig the big plastic bags of popcorn out of the trash. We'd fill our bellies and then drag the bags home, saving the rest for later. Often, it would be the only food we'd have for days at a time. The cast-off popcorn filled my aching belly and got me through a lot of hungry nights. My mouth still waters at its sweet smell. Popcorn is my favorite food group; I grab a bag or a handful whenever I get a chance, as though someday the world might run out of it and I'd never get another taste.

When begging didn't work, and when none of my other sources came through, then I'd turn to sack-lunch larceny. I don't remember exactly when Our Lady of Sorrows Grade School stopped serving free hot meals, but it was then that my classmates began complaining that their sack lunches were disappearing. I'd watch where the other kids stashed their brown bags and box lunches in the coatroom before the starting bell. I'd try to resist the temptation to steal, just like the nuns and brothers taught, but when my prayers for a Big Mac miracle went unanswered, and my belly had gone empty for a day and a half, the predatory instincts took over. My favorite ploy was to hang back on the playground so that I was the last one in the coatroom each morning. I'd swipe a brown bag fat with promise from under a hat or coat and put it beneath my own. At lunchtime, I'd dash into the coatroom, grab the sack, and sprint back to the lunch table so that I'd be halfway through someone else's bologna and cheese before the alarm was sounded. Often I'd get caught, but with a sandwich in my belly the punishment was irrelevant. If someone threatened to take my stolen meal before I'd wolfed it down, I made it clear that the next bite might come from their behind.

We can laugh about those days now, but sometimes Dear will get tears in her eyes when we talk about how hungry we were. Years later, after I'd signed with the Pistons and used my bonus money to buy her a house in the suburbs, we were sitting around the breakfast table, thinking of those days. Then Dear brought out platter after platter of eggs, bacon, ham, sausage, and grits, and we laughed like madmen at the ridiculous amount of food. I told her that I couldn't eat. There was too much food to choose from after all those lean years. It was easier to make a choice when all we had was grease sandwiches. That's right, two pieces of bread rubbed over the previous day's frying pan, slapped together and eaten. It was a feast in those days.

THE CHOICE BETWEEN DREAMS AND DESPAIR

Hunger and poverty create a ripe environment for dreams but they just as easily can trigger despair. The course of your life is determined by whether you buy into your aspirations or your desperation. I was fortunate in having a mother who never stopped dreaming of the possibilities in spite of our family's often desperate circumstances. Her refusal to accept poverty as a permanent condition and her unwavering belief in the power of dreams were my mother's greatest gift to us. That, and her unconditional love. We had little other than love and our dreams. For a time, after my father left the house, we were a nomadic tribe, living in tenement apartments, abandoned buildings, and slum houses, always moving to stay ahead of bill collectors and landlords. Yet, my mother instilled in us this sense that we were really princes and princesses living in a temporary state of poverty. She thought that if we felt superior to our circumstances, we wouldn't fall prey to them.

So many around us did. I can't tell you how many friends I saw die. I've tried to bury those memories someplace deep in my soul, a place I don't visit often. I'd rather not have those thoughts, but they do come. It would happen so fast. You'd be with someone, leave them for a few minutes, come back, and he'd be dead. Gone forever. It would happen and be over so quick that you sometimes wondered if the person had ever existed outside your imagination. You become almost numb to it. You see so many people get shot or killed that it becomes part of your everyday existence. You may become hardened to the loss of friends and schoolmates, but I've never forgotten the deaths I've witnessed. I was only twelve years old when I came upon one of my brother's friends at the bottom of the stairs, dying, with a hypodermic needle still spiked in his forearm. He'd stumbled out of the upstairs bathroom and fallen, probably because of an air bubble in his vein, but you never know. There was a lot of bad stuff around the West Side in those days. Dealers were cutting heroin with everything from baking soda to Nestlé's Quik. Everyone in the house heard him go down the wood stairs. I got there first, and I started slapping him in the face and pounding on his chest, trying to revive him. People don't die like you see on television. It's the ugliest thing, watching the person trying to hold on and then shaking, grabbing that last breath and going. . . . When I think about those I've seen die, it takes me into dark places that I prefer not to visit.

PREDATOR OR PREY

Drugs, alcohol, guns, and gangs didn't allow for much innocence in my childhood. You were predator or potential prey. Not all of my physical scars were inflicted on the basketball court. There were periods when I fought my way to school and then back home every day for weeks. I fought this one kid—I never even knew his name—every time we ran into each other. No words were spoken. Each time, we fought until we were exhausted. I don't know why. He probably didn't either. We moved around so much from one neighborhood to another that I was always fighting just to prove that I wasn't weak. I lost as many fights as I won, but the motto was "You have to take some to get some." To get in a punch, you had to get in close enough and take a few.

My mother couldn't protect me from everything, though she certainly did her best. Through sheer force of will, she kept all nine of us in Catholic private school and out of public housing. She believed it was the only way we could survive. Even now she becomes emotional when she talks about those times. "We were living at 3340 West Congress Parkway and I was on ADC [Aid to Dependent Children] and welfare, and my caseworker wanted me to move my family into the projects. She said I couldn't stay on welfare and live in private housing," my mother recalled. "I tried to talk to her about it and tell her I didn't want to take my boys into the projects because of all the gangs and drugs, but she wouldn't listen."

The caseworker did not take into account my mother's fierce devotion to her dreams for us. I was only about ten years old, but I remember how upset she was over being forced to move into "one of those damn hellhole projects." She left one day without telling us where she was going. Anyone who says you can't fight city hall has yet to run up against Mary Thomas.

"I've always been a strong-willed person. I'd never met Mayor [Richard J.] Daley, but I went to his office. I knew there had to be somebody who could help me with the struggle in raising my kids," she recalled. "When I got there, the lady at the front desk said I couldn't see the mayor. I told her it was very important and I started to tell her what I was going to do in that office if she didn't let me talk to him. Before I got the words out, Mayor Daley stepped out and said to let me in.

"I told him that I did not want to move my family into the projects, where there was nothing but gangs and fighting. I said I had seven boys and I wanted to keep them away from gangs by staying where I was. He listened but he never said a word. He just looked at me. So when I finished I got up and thanked him for listening and I walked out."

The next day, my family's welfare caseworker called my mother on the telephone. She started to give my mother hell for going to the mayor. "She told me I was crazy for thinking it would do any good, but I interrupted her and asked if the mayor had called her about me. She said that he had. Then her supervisor cut in and said, 'The mayor said you don't have to move into the projects.' I then told the supervisor, 'Well, tell that other heifer it must have done a *whole* lot of good to go see the mayor.'"

My mother fought off bureaucrats, bill collectors, and gang members to keep her dreams for us alive. Of course, the gangs weren't restricted to the projects, so they weren't easy to avoid even if you didn't live there. The Vice Lords controlled most of our neighborhood. When they held their annual parade, marching down Holman Avenue to Madison Street, no one dared stand and watch. The streets were abandoned to them. Dear knew the gang leaders and most of the members, and they knew her from the youth center. She was the neighborhood's unofficial juvenile advocate. She often went to court and testified on behalf of kids from the neighborhood. Many times, she'd bail them out of the Audy Home juvenile detention center by posting bond or giving her word that they'd stay out of trouble until their trial dates. She was respected as a force to be reckoned with in our neighborhood. It was a well-earned reputation.

THE THOMAS GANG

One day when I was six years old, the Vice Lords staged a raid on our rented place on Congress Parkway. I'm not sure what set them off. My mother and sister Ruby say it was an annual recruitment day for new gang members. Lord Henry disputes that. He says they don't know the real story because he never told them the truth. The Vice Lords were looking for him and what he'd stolen from them, he said. Lord Henry was into drugs back then. And he had stolen eight ounces of heroin from a shipment that the gang was going to distribute. "I was corrupt then. I was already an addict, but our mother didn't know it," he told me.

For whatever reason, the Vice Lords came calling that day. They poured in through the windows from the fire escape, through the door, and, it seemed, up through the plumbing and cracks in the floor. They were threatening to kidnap or hurt my brothers if they didn't get what they wanted. Someone must have tipped off Dear, because she was prepared for the invasion. Nobody in the family had ever seen the sawed-off twelve-gauge she pulled out from under the sink that day. But she leveled it at the gang members like Dirty Harry in a housedress. Dear threatened to blow very specific body parts across the Eisenhower Expressway if they didn't get out. "There ain't but one gang in this family, and that's the Thomas gang, and I'm its leader," she told them. Clint Eastwood could not have delivered the lines any more convincingly.

I know. It does sound like a made-for-TV movie—and it was. HBO included that incident in a made-for-TV version of our family story called *A Mother's Courage, The Mary Thomas Story*. Dear stood her ground and the gangs backed off. Most gang members knew and respected my mother and that is really what saved our skins, not only that time but countless others. People have a black-and-white version of life in the ghetto, but there's more gray than most imagine. Not all gang members are full-time, heartless killers. Pimps, drug dealers, hookers, and thieves have their own codes of honor. Personal courage and family bonds were still respected in my neighborhood in those days, perhaps more than in more affluent areas of the city, or in the boardrooms of business.

It was clear to the Vice Lords that my mother was willing to die to protect her dreams. Many of them no doubt wished their own parents had been so tenacious and so involved in their lives. They left that day and many of them came back to our house after that to seek temporary shelter. For all of my childhood, our home, wherever it was, served as an unofficial refuge or sanctuary guarded by "Mama Thom." Members of opposing gangs would come to our house to sleep, maybe to eat if there happened to be any scraps of food around. We were taught to share what little we had. My mother didn't allow them to bring in drugs or guns. Even powerful gang leaders like Willie Lord of the Vice Lords and Pee Wee, leader of the rival Black Souls, became regular visitors.

RISING ABOVE OUR SURROUNDINGS

Willie, who I believe is now in prison, respected my mother's strength and devotion to family and, to a certain extent, he and other gang members bought into her dreams for us. I can't tell you exactly how often a member of my family received a pass on the streets after being recognized as one of Mama Thom's kids. It happened many, many times to me, and to others in my family. In spite of all the despair around us, she dreamed of better things for us, and she convinced everyone from the mayor of Chicago to some of the toughest gang members on the West Side to believe in it too. I don't know just how Dear did it, but we grew up with the sense that we were destined for better things, and she seemed to get others to buy into it as well. She and my father always had admired the closeness of the Kennedy family and their emphasis on togetherness and education. She led us to believe that we were the Kennedy clan of our neighborhood.

I'll never forget the first time a classmate accused me of arrogance. I was shocked. I went home and asked my mother if it was true. My sister laughed when she heard me. "Of course we're arrogant. Dear wired it into our personalities." We may have lived several notches below the poverty line, but we believed we were destined for the penthouse. The path to it, we were always told, was through knowledge. When my father, Isiah Thomas II, was with the family, he was adamant that we develop our minds. My parents both grew up poor in the South. Both dealt with racism and discrimination. They believed in education as the way to rise above it. They had little tolerance for laggards. We were rarely allowed to watch anything but PBS or other "educational" programming on television when my parents were around. Ruby did get around the rules by watching the soap operas on the Spanish channels. She'd tell my mother she was doing it to learn the language. Whether that was really her plan or just an excuse, it worked. Today she is a high school Spanish teacher.

My father hated most of what was on television. He didn't even watch sports because he saw black athletes as "entertainers" playing for the amusement of whites. He never went to my brothers' games, and we weren't allowed to watch sports on television when he was around. Instead, he encouraged us to read and discuss issues, the news, and world events. He wanted us to be doctors, lawyers, and leaders who could change the world, so he expected us to know how it worked—at least *his* perception of how it worked.

He demanded that my brothers and sisters make "reports" around the dinner table at night. We may not have had much to eat, but we had our family discussions at the table anyway. We had to have something to say about a book that we were reading, a news event, a topic from school, or a subject from the old set of encyclopedias my father kept. There were often heated arguments that didn't end until everyone agreed that my father was right. He was a man of very strong opinions, particularly on racial matters. His usual debate opponent was Ruby, who is every bit as opinionated and tough minded. She was the first in the family to go to college, and she wasn't afraid to take on my father, who secretly admired her fire. In the 1960s, Ruby supported Dr. Martin Luther King Jr. and his nonviolent approach to fighting discrimination. My father was more militant. He supported Malcolm X. He thought King's peaceful demonstrations were a waste of time, and that King was a pawn of the white establishment. My other brothers and sisters would sit back and listen for hours as Ruby and my father went back and forth on that topic. My family still talks about the fury that Ruby provoked when she insisted to my father that Jesus was white. And they laugh too about the time my father announced that no one in the family was to use the term "Negro" ever again. "We are African-Americans, just as the Italians are Italian-Americans and the Mexicans are Mexican-Americans," he said. "Our ancestors came from the African continent, so we are African-Americans." When someone in the family tried to argue for the continued use of the forbidden word, my father angrily got out an old globe, pointed to it, and commanded: "Find me the country here named 'Negro!'"

I was too young to participate in most of these nightly sessions when my father was around, but the tradition continued even after he left. My performance in each high school game. My grades. My options for college. Who I was hanging out with. Every aspect of my life was the subject of scrutiny and debate at these family caucuses. Even today, when there is a family crisis or an important decision to be made, we gather around a table and have at it. Because of my family's emphasis on achievement, I always knew that playing basketball would never be all that I did with my life. I dreamed of playing in the NBA, but I was expected to do more with my life. I wasn't very old when my family started talking about me being a lawyer or politician. For a long time, law school was the real dream for me. I played basketball because I loved it, and because it offered a way into college and a better life for all of us.

DREAMS GIVE BIRTH TO ACHIEVEMENT

My parents, and especially my mother, understood that the deadliest killer in our neighborhood was not drugs, street gangs, or the lack of nourishment; it was a poverty of dreams. If you can't dream of better times ahead, then you are bound to fall to the despair of your present plight. All of us were taught that although we lived in the ghetto, it did not have to live within us. There were many in our neighborhood who had difficulty seeing beyond their circumstances. Several of my brothers were among them. Preston and Gregory battled with addiction and finally overcame it, but Ronnie died just a few years ago, after many years of struggling with alcoholism. Some have been in and out of drug rehabilitation and in and out of jail. Yet, even as despair stunted their lives, they joined forces to keep me out of harm's way. My success is due in large part to the power of my family's shared mission to see that at least one of us would rise to the level of our mother's dreams—and pull her up and out of the ghetto with us.

Not that I am the only "success" in my family. Ruby is a well-regarded teacher in the Chicago public school system. Mark is a veteran Chicago police officer, and Lord Henry has been winning a long, long battle with drug dependency. I am particularly proud of my oldest brother because of the obstacles he had to overcome. He certainly had it tougher than me, in no small part because he and my other brothers protected me and told me to learn from their examples, both good and bad. "You were exposed to the thrill of drug use, and the tragic parts of it too," Lord Henry recently told me. It's true: I was never drawn to get high, because long before drugs were ever offered to me, I saw the tragic lows and the destruction of my brothers' dreams.

LORD HENRY'S LOST DREAMS

People from the old neighborhood still talk about Lord Henry's basketball skills. He played with such a fluid grace, it was like watching tai chi. They called him "Rat," which he has never much liked, because he was lightning fast. He could mask his speed by changing the rhythm of his movements. It often seemed like he'd be at one spot on the court and then vanish and appear somewhere else. In my playing days, sportswriters would occasionally comment on my "deceptive quickness." It came from Lord Henry.

He played at St. Philip High School in Chicago. It was a private school and they had only a couple black players back then. I started going to his games as soon as I was old enough to walk. I'd watch him and practice his moves on the sidelines or in the stands. He was an unstoppable player who easily could have gone on to college and the pros. But he got into drugs and gang-banging. He hid it from Dear and most of us, but he was using from an early age. He told me not long ago that he used heroin and cocaine for more than twenty-five years. He's now fifty and he's been drug-free for about ten years. He's worked in drug counseling, and when Lord Henry tells people about how drugs can destroy dreams, he knows what he is talking about.

Ruby says that a Chicago cop once told her that Lord Henry was the "classiest drug addict" he had ever known. That's not exactly an honor that anyone should aspire to, but it was a good description of my brother. During his many years of drug abuse, he and the beat cops who usually chased him had sort of a friendly rivalry. He was not a violent guy, except when he or someone close to him was threatened. He never fought the police; he was more of a "runner," and a particularly elusive one.

To look at Lord Henry today, you would never know that he had been a drug addict for decades, unless he shows you the track marks on his arms. He is amazingly fit and looks ten years younger than he actually is. He attributes his youthfulness, in part, to his years of dodging the law. "I had a regular escape route when the cops were chasing me. I'd run up to the eighth floor of this big apartment building and jump off the roof to the building next door and go into it," Lord Henry recalled. "I had to stay in shape to be able to do that, so I'd run those stairs four or five times a week, just so I'd be able to do it when I was being chased."

The West Side beat cops would occasionally get frustrated that they couldn't catch him on foot, so they'd try other tactics, he said. "One time Officer Cromie, who was always chasing me, was looking for me with some federal drug agents for some reason. They pulled up to me at a street corner and there were three guys in the squad instead of the usual two, so I knew something was up. I took off running and they chased me in the car onto a schoolyard. They were running me all over this playground and I realized that they were just trying to wear me out, so I jumped the fence and took off. I got a couple blocks away and figured I'd lost them. I turned and looked back and they were still parked in the schoolyard. I thought I'd ditched them. But then the back door of the squad opened, and out stepped this young Korean guy. He was wearing a track suit and running shoes. He pointed at me and laughed and I thought, 'Oh no, they brought in a speedster with fresh legs.' I took off again, but I swear I only got about ten steps before he grabbed me from behind."

Lord Henry managed to avoid any serious run-ins with the law, but his life was difficult. He was shot at two or three times in gang fights and hit once. The bullet went through one leg and lodged deeply in his foot. It stayed there for a couple years before "it worked its way out," he said. One day he was standing at a bus stop when someone opened fire with a shotgun. He had no time to react. He stood there as pellets blasted into the brick building behind him, but he was not even scratched. "They used to call me the luckiest guy on the West Side," he said.

Like most in my family, Lord Henry is a naturally upbeat guy, but in truth, there was nothing charmed about his life. The curse of his addiction robbed him of his athletic promise and his ability to earn a living, and it led him to do things that he still feels ashamed of. Over the years, I offered to help him anytime he was ready. He tried drug rehabilitation programs several different times, but always he went back to using. I've learned the hard way that you can only help Lord Henry and others like him when they are ready to help themselves. It wasn't until about eleven years ago that Lord Henry told our mother that he was tired of the life he'd fallen into but uncertain about how he could finally escape it. I found him on a Sunday night. He was standing on a corner, smoking crack and, he later admitted, planning a robbery. I pulled up in a car, rolled down the window, and called his name. It took nearly a minute for him to hear it through the narcotic fog. He looked at me with dull eyes and I asked him, "Are you ready?"

"Yeah," he said.

I told him that I'd be sending someone for him. Lord Henry said he'd be ready for him. Several days later, our brother Mark, the policeman, escorted Lord Henry out of the old neighborhood, onto a plane to Detroit and a drug treatment center that I'd signed him into. He says that marked the beginning of his "new life" and the return of his ability to dream of better things.

A DREAM DIVERTED

Lord Henry was not the only one of my brothers to lose track of his dreams. Larry was also a great athlete. He played basketball for Wright Junior College after high school and he did so well he was asked to come to a tryout for the Bulls. But just before the big day he suffered a severe ankle injury that ended his season and his prospects for a pro career. It was a major disappointment for him, and he turned to other, less legitimate opportunities. He became a street hustler, running games and running women. Larry became a pimp. That's about as bluntly and truthfully as I can put it. He was a great athlete, a good guy, a caring brother and son, a hustler, a smooth operator, and a very successful pimp—at least until my mother got wind of it; then he became sort of semiretired.

Lord Henry's basketball career ended before I was old enough to fully appreciate it firsthand. But I'd been able to follow Larry's grade school, high school, and college games. He was my hero on and off the court. I used to do a halftime show at his games at Our Lady of Sorrows when I was only three years old. I had my own uniform jersey and I'd dribble out on the floor and imitate Larry's moves. Later, he helped get me into a summer league for thirteen- and fourteen-year-olds, even though I was only eight. Larry used to carry me to games on his shoulders so that I wouldn't get my shoes wet in the snow.

When I was in the seventh grade, I was so fascinated with him that I'd go into his room when he wasn't around and look at his things, especially his clothes. Larry was into the *Superfly* look, which I thought was very cool too. One morning when he was out taking care of business, I got into Larry's closet and put together an ensemble for school. It included a pair of hot-pink bell-bottoms, a pink and white shirt, white shoes, and a big old hat with a feather in it. Dennis Rodman would have been *extremely* jealous. My brother was not amused. He was cruising by in his powder-blue Cadillac as I walked to school. He recognized the clothes before he recognized me, then he dragged my bell-bottomed butt back home.

What followed was the first of many brother-on-brother counseling sessions designed to keep me out of the sort of trouble that many of my brothers had already experienced. Larry held a bag of heroin in my face and advised me that "this stuff can kill you." He also told me that the best way to win the hustler's game was to refuse to play it. "Don't play and you can't lose," he said. It was a critical point in my life. I could have gone either way. Larry stopped me from choosing the wrong path. He told me that he hated the way his life was turning out. He felt he had blown his opportunity, but he would not stand by and watch me do it. "Somebody has got to get the NBA pay-check," he said. "Lord Henry failed to make it to the pros. So did Gregory. I was *that* close to it, and I failed. We owe it to ourselves. Somebody has got to get that money."

Larry may well have saved my life. He stepped in and gave me the guidance I needed at that point. He helped me see that the quick returns offered by the street simply didn't compare to the long-term benefits of staying clean and focusing on basketball. "We live the way we do because we have to, not because we want to," he and Lord Henry told me, in somewhat stronger language. "This is not the way you should want to live or be."

They were telling me that while they may have fallen off the course to their own dreams, their hopes for me were still alive. And they were not going to allow them to easily die. Their belief in me gave me strength. Make no mistake, I was never a saint. There were many times when I wanted to take an easier route or go for a quick score rather than stick with their plans for me. But they kept me on course through intimidation, through force, through love. With their help, I came to understand the power of choosing dreams over despair and fear.

FUNDAMENTAL POINTS

- While your eyes might be able to see only what is going on around you right now, your imagination and your dreams can open your mind to the possibilities of a better life.

- Dreams help you form a vision for your life—not the life that poverty or prejudice would set out for you, but one that you determine for yourself. Dreams give you reason to have hope. They open your eyes to better things. They give you a path to walk.

- Once you envision the life that you want in your dreams, you can then set realistic goals that will lead you there in the real world.

2.

MEASURE AT THE ROOT

I was named the *Sporting News* Rookie of the Year in my first season with the Detroit Pistons in 1982, but I didn't take the summer off to relax and bask in a successful start to my NBA career. You might expect that of a twenty-year-old ghetto kid with more than just a few pennies in his pocket for the first time in his life. Instead of hitting the beach and resting on my laurels that summer, I hit the books. You see, I signed *two* contracts after leaving college at the end of my sophomore year. The first contract was with the Detroit Pistons. The second was with my mother. I don't have to tell you which of them was the toughest to negotiate.

When I left Indiana University after only two years to enter the NBA draft, I promised my mother—and myself—that I would earn my college degree in the off-season. The contract with Dear was a legally binding agreement. It said that even though I'd left college to turn pro, I would still get my college degree. I had a lawyer draw it up and both Dear and I signed it. There was even a penalty for failing to fulfill the agreement. If I didn't finish college within a certain length of time, I would have to give my mother *all* the money I'd earned as a pro player up to that point. It took nearly six years of class work and studies in the off-season before I got my degree, thus avoiding an ugly courtroom confrontation with my mother. (In some ways, that's too bad. It would have made for an interesting show for *Judge Judy* or *Court TV*.)

No doubt about it, there were many summer afternoons when I'd have much rather been hanging out by the pool or playing golf than sitting in a hot and stuffy classroom. I was seriously tempted to skip class and head out for the golf course. But I didn't have to search deep in my memory to grasp what happens to those people who give up long-term goals for short-term gratification. I'm not condemning them. They aren't bad or evil people. Most of them were not given many, if any, opportunities to escape the circumstances they were born into. I was lucky to have parents and family members who believed in setting high goals. I was even luckier in that I had a lot of help, support, pushes, and shoves from people who cared deeply about me. Family members, coaches, teachers, guidance counselors, and others drummed into me the importance of having goals as I was growing up. I'm grateful for that. It helped to make me an extremely goal-oriented person. I have never stopped dreaming as a result, and I've never stopped setting goals to help me achieve those dreams. Getting a good education was my goal as a boy. My mother drummed that one into me and it became the measure of everything I did. Playing basketball was a joy, but I always saw it as a diversion—until it became a way to get a college scholarship and continue my education. You see, you can have all sorts of goals. Winning the NCAA championship was surely a big goal when I was at Indiana University. But it was not my primary goal, or even the most important secondary goal. My most urgent goal at the time was to build enough wealth to give my mother the security and comfort that she had earned in all her years of sacrifice. That is why I left Indiana after my sophomore year and took the hardship option so that I could enter the NBA draft. But once my *most urgent* goal was accomplished,

I returned to working on my *root* goal—to complete my degree so that I could contribute something to the world once my basketball career was over. Even through my pro years, I kept my eyes on that bigger goal. Today I'm certainly focused on bringing an NBA championship to the Indiana Pacers franchise and the fans who support us. But I have never lost track of my long-term goal, which is to own an NBA franchise myself so that I can open doors and provide opportunities for others like me.

DRIVING TOWARD THE GOAL

Setting goals—for both the short term and long term—and going after them is critical to having a successful life. Nearly every decision I made as a young man, and now as an adult, was based on whether or not it moved me closer to my goals. You wouldn't start building a house without having a blueprint, would you? You wouldn't plan a long trip without checking the map. I wouldn't send my Pacers players onto the court without a game plan. So why would you live without at least some general goals based on what you want and what is most important to you?

Have you ever heard the saying, "It's not the destination that counts, it's the journey"? Life is a journey. You want to enjoy as much of it as you can because when you reach the end of it . . . well, I don't know about you, but I'd rather go down into the ground with every ounce of my energy and talents used up. It's the journey that counts, and goals are your mile markers along the way. They determine the course you follow in your personal life, your work or career, and in your relationships with others.

How do you decide what your goals are going to be? One method is to think about the people whose accomplishments you most admire. What can you do to make your life as fulfilling or meaningful as theirs? Dear was my biggest hero because she gave so much to her family and community even though she had very little. I also looked up to Muhammad Ali because he always stood by what he believed in, even when it wasn't the most popular thing to do. While having role models is important—I'll tell you more about this later—it is vital that you set goals based on what you want for your own life, not just to please or impress other people. That's known as "putting your ladder against the wrong wall," because one day you'll reach the top rung only to realize you aren't where you really want to be. To prevent that from happening, you might try envisioning yourself at different points in the future, five, ten, twenty, thirty, and forty years down the road. Think of where you'd like to be and what you'd like to be doing at each point in your life, then set your goals accordingly.

In my discussions with other athletes, coaches, and business and community leaders, I've seen time and time again that to enjoy long-term and lasting success, you must constantly measure your progress in life by measuring "at the root," or according to the most important—most deeply rooted—goals that you've set. People who always measure their progress by these primary or "root" goals are not afraid to fail or face challenges. They are unrelenting. If one path to their goal is blocked, they try another. If one door closes, they immediately begin searching for one that is open. If one goal is accomplished, they set another. The great Olympian Jackie Joyner-Kersee was so much better than any of her competitors that she had to challenge herself by setting higher and higher goals all the time. "I always had something to shoot for each year; to jump one inch farther," she once said. Jackie set fresh goals with each new track season.

What do you do if your life isn't built around a sports season? When is it time for you to set new goals? Certainly it's time to do that if you have accomplished a short-term or even a long-term goal. You might also look to set new and higher goals each time you change jobs, start or end a relationship, bring a new person into your family, move to a new location, or any other time when there is an opportunity to harness the positive momentum of a change in your life.

One way to add to that momentum and make sure you take your goals seriously is to write them down and keep them in a place where you can review them regularly—maybe on a night-stand next to your bed, or taped to the bathroom mirror. There is something about putting a goal on paper that validates it and gives it power. If you write them down and keep them where you can see them or refer to them often, your goals will translate into actions and accomplishments. There is nothing easy about achieving your dreams, but by setting goals and constantly work-ing toward them in spite of distractions and frustrations, your life will pick up positive momentum.

GOALS AS STEPPING-STONES

In my family, we were taught to establish goals and to have a vision for our lives built around them. Those who never lost focus on their root goals succeeded in escaping poverty and despair. But those who lost track of their most important goals struggled to make it. Dear encouraged each of us to keep those long-term goals in our minds and to review them when making critical choices. To this day, when I face a difficult decision, I remind myself to "measure at the root." It's my way of remem-bering that I've got a mission for my life. I'm not certain where the phrase "measure at the root" originated, but my guess is that it has something to do with gauging the full size or true health of a plant by checking the depth of its roots. The tree with shallow roots is easily toppled. The same applies to a life that has no deeply rooted goals. I've found also that the best way to make important decisions is to look at how each alternative choice measures against your long-term plans and principles.

I've been blessed in that I've been able to achieve many of my goals so far, but I don't measure my success in terms of the money or material things I've accumulated. The real measure of success is your ability to keep growing by seeking new challenges, looking for new opportunities, and setting even higher and more ambitious goals while also making sure you measure your progress against your ultimate, long-term, most deeply rooted goals. A friend of mine said that every time he and his brothers and sister visited his father's office as a child, his father would have him stand against the wall behind a door. The father would then put a ruler from the top of each child's head to the wall, marking his or her height and writing the date beside it. My friend and his brothers and sisters could then always measure how much they'd grown with each visit to their father's office. It is important to do the same sort of thing as you grow in your career and in your life in general. I'm always reviewing where I've been, how far I've come, and where I want to go, measuring those factors in light of my overall goals and aspirations for my life. It's my way of staying focused on what is most important to me.

My parents had high expectations in spite of our low circumstances. My mother worked herself into poor health to guarantee that we had the opportunity to get good educations. She preached the value of learning to us every night. She demanded that we have our homework done before bedtime at 8:00 p.m., but it wasn't unusual for her to wake us up, quiz us on what we'd studied, and make us go over the material again if our answers weren't satisfactory.

My brothers and sisters also pushed me to keep my grades up, even sometimes when they were struggling in their own efforts to stay in school. Since Dear worked and couldn't afford day care or a baby-sitter, I had to go to school when Preston started. So, I was three years old when I began attending kindergarten. I wasn't an official student, but they treated me like one. I usually did whatever my brother and the rest of the class was doing. I was way ahead of the other kids my age when I finally became a legitimate student. I'd also absorbed a lot of information while sitting around the homework table with my brothers and sisters. By the time a teacher presented material to me in class, chances were that I'd already been through it a couple of times at home. Hunger pangs and fights over food led to most of my problems in grade school, where I was thrown out for fighting more than once.

High school was a different matter. At first, I felt like I didn't belong in the world as it existed at St. Joseph's High School. I'd wanted to go to a public school—one where most of my friends had gone. Instead, they'd made me come miles away from home to where I felt isolated and unwanted. At first, I resented the fact that most of the other guys at St. Joe's had money for food and nice clothes. I came to school hungry most days. And the clothes I wore depended on what was left after everyone else had grabbed their shirts, pants, shoes, and socks. That's how it worked at my house, but I still felt self-conscious about it. Even my coach teased me about my mismatched socks all the time. "Did you get dressed in the dark again, Isiah?"

I lived in a different world and at first I was real self-conscious about it. A white face was a rarity in my own neighborhood. White suburbia, with all of its strange habits and easy comforts, was a foreign environment to me. I didn't look like anybody. I didn't dress like anybody. I didn't know anybody. And it frosted my shorts (literally) that at first, none of them offered to give me a ride when they drove by me as I walked from the bus stop in snow up to my knees. I missed my friends and my own world. I might as well have been a foreign exchange student at St. Joseph's. When I did try to fit in a little, I took crap from my brothers or friends in the neighborhood for acting or talking like a white guy.

My freshman year marked the first year that a big group of black students was admitted to St. Joseph's. There weren't any mass protests like at Little Rock or Selma, but there were a few incidents and a couple times when I had to take off running from carloads of racists making threats. It didn't last for long, and eventually I came to enjoy the school, but at first I was not at all happy to be there.

DEEPLY ROOTED GOALS KEEP YOU ON COURSE

"I'm quitting this school," I told my mother on the phone.

It was near the beginning of my freshman year at St. Joseph's, a Catholic, all-boys school in Westchester, a predominately white suburb that was at least a one-and-a-half-hour bus ride and a one-and-a-half-mile walk from wherever we happened to be living on Chicago's West Side. I had to get up at five-thirty in the morning to catch the first bus on school days. It was usually dark and cold as a killer's heart. I'd sit in the bus and watch the sun come up, so that by the time I got off to start walking the rest of the way, it seemed like I'd been riding all day. When I called my mother to tell her I was quitting, I'd been late again. I'd been disciplined again, and I was sick of it all. I felt as though my brothers had all but kidnapped me and sold me off.

"Junior, you do what you think is right," my mother said calmly on the phone after I called to bail out of St. Joe's. "But tell me again what your plan is, and say it slowly."

"I'm quitting," I said in irritation.

I knew what was coming next.

"Slower, say it slower," Dear said patiently.

It was no use. I'd been down this dead-end path before. There wasn't an army on earth that could outlast her resolve to keep me in that school.

"I'm . . . staying."

I surrendered.

There was no room for compromise in my mother's belief that education was the way out of poverty. Through hell or high water, she'd put every one of us through Catholic private school because she believed "my children are too good for public schools." They didn't come any poorer or any prouder than my Dear. And no one was more dedicated to achieving her goals for her children. I shared her goals for me, but sometimes she and my other family members had to set me straight and back on course.

SHARED GOALS LEAD TO SHARED SUCCESS

Most of my brothers attended St. Philip High School, a Catholic League school, but it had closed its doors by the time I reached high school age. I lobbied to go to one of the powerhouse basketball schools and my brothers went around to several of them trying to get me admitted on an athletic or hardship scholarship. I had played real well in a summer tournament against a bunch of guys headed for one big Catholic school, but when my brother Larry asked their coach if he'd be interested in having me, the guy said, "He's good, but he's too short." A few years later, when I was leading St. Joseph's to the finals of the state tournament, Larry ran into the same coach. "What do you think now," Larry teased him. "If I turn around and bend over, would you please kick me?" the coach said.

The only Catholic school coach who was even mildly interested was St. Joseph's. Coach Gene Pingatore had seen me play. He thought I had potential in spite of my size and lack of discipline. Mr. Pingatore, which is what I've always called him, is a lot like Bobby Knight. He is a no-nonsense disciplinarian who coaches defense, defense, and more defense. Offense was considered a necessary evil. Mr. Pingatore is one of the good guys, but he could play a very convincing tough guy too. Of course, my mother thought he was terrific. She could be the national spokesperson for the "tough love" approach to coaching, and parenting too.

It took me a while to adjust to Mr. Pingatore and his philosophy. He saw me as a diamond in the rough. I thought I was pretty dazzling already. In truth, I was capable of dominating practices and games, so at first I took every opportunity to do that. Mr. Pingatore recalls that I tended to treat an in-bounds pass as an assist. I'd get the pass, dribble all the way downcourt, and shoot. He had to enlighten me as to the other options available, such as passing to a teammate. What can I say? I was young and loose and full of juice. I felt I had to prove myself as a one-on-one player—particularly because of my size. Mr. Pingatore, like all good coaches, wanted to mold me into a team player. Our goals were different and so we warred with each other until I finally saw that it wasn't about me, it was about the team. I might have racked up some impressive stats as a scoring machine, but my team wasn't going to win a lot of games that way. Mr. Pingatore showed me that if I wanted to be a winner, I had to be a team player. When I saw the light and made that my goal, the Chargers began winning consistently.

Mr. Pingatore was also a stickler for performance in the classroom and he rode me hard about my studies. I struggled with my studies in my freshman year. By the time I made the long bus and trek to class—often without having had any breakfast—I was often worn out. The whole experience was disorienting to me.

I had to make some big adjustments for a thirteen-year-old kid. The biggest was in the classroom. I'd always been a good student but I had a difficult time focusing on studies at first. In the final semester of my freshman year, I got an F in algebra and I finished the year with an overall D average. Mr. Pingatore and my mother were all over me. They said that I'd never get to play beyond high school if I couldn't pass the academic standards. I had to go to summer school to bring my grades back up so that I'd be eligible to play my sophomore year. I told them that I would never again let my grades slip so low, and by my senior year I was on the honor roll.

LIVING PEAK TO PEAK

My family came to every high school game and my brothers made me replay every perceived mistake afterward. They were relentless. In one game my sophomore year, my jump shots were banging off the front of the rim like beer cans on a curb. As soon as I got home, still wet from the postgame shower, they dragged me outside in the snow and made me shoot until my fingers went numb and the rubber in the ball started to crack.

I wasn't exactly thrilled at the frostbite back then, but I'll never forget their dedication and support. It was my great luck to have a family that was always measuring my progress at the root—according to the goals they'd set for me. My sisters and brothers didn't push me because they wanted a piece of the action later. Nor was it about *my* success. It was always about getting our mother out of the ghetto, providing her with security and comfort in her later years. That was the ultimate goal in our family. We loved and cared about each other. We have never abandoned each other. But Dear came first for us, because she has always put us first.

There were so many great athletes in my old neighborhood, so many smart, shrewd, energetic, and charismatic people. I escaped because my family set one goal after another for me and made sure that as soon as I accomplished one goal I got on to the next. That's called *living peak to peak*. You climb one mountain and then look for a higher one. It was never in doubt that the real purpose for going to St. Joe's was to prepare for my college education and life after basketball. Even then, my success model was not built on sports. My mother and sisters, in particular, made it clear that if I didn't get a college education, my basketball accomplishments didn't mean a thing.

In fact, they didn't think I really had much of a chance at all for a basketball scholarship. I struggled as a sophomore in my first year on the varsity team, and it looked so bad, my mother and Ruby told me one night that they had no idea how they were ever going to pay my way to college. We'd been talking about my dream of being a lawyer who would work for poor people. They told me that if I didn't get into college somehow, I was more likely to be one of the poor people than a lawyer.

Then, in my junior year, the St. Joe's team came together. Mr. Pingatore had taken a lot of the showboat out of my game. He taught me to focus more on defense and team play. It worked. I started getting a lot of media attention, and suddenly the stands were more crowded. Scouts and coaches from Iowa, Illinois, Indiana, Michigan, Notre Dame, and other major colleges began showing up. My mother couldn't believe it. She called Mr. Pingatore after reading one newspaper story about my potential as a college player. "Do you really think Junior might be able to get a basketball scholarship to some small school somewhere?"

The coach laughed into the phone. Then he told Dear he'd come to the house that night and show her a few things. He came with three big boxes, each full of letters from colleges and coaches around the country, all of whom were interested in offering me a basketball scholarship.

"I can't believe you are worried about him getting a scholarship," coach said. "His problem is going to be in choosing which one to take. And this is only the beginning of your headache. Wait until next season, when he's a senior!"

My mother knew I was a good basketball player, but my brothers had all been good basketball players too. She and the rest of the family had devoted themselves to keeping me on track with my studies as well as my game. They were so focused on the academics that they had not realized how far my playing had advanced. My family was heavily invested in my success. In many ways, I was the last hope. There was a tremendous amount of pressure on me to succeed both athletically and academically. Everything I did, every decision I made had to take that goal into account.

Neither my mother nor I ever envisioned high school or college as a mere training ground for basketball. You can only play a game so long, then you have to do something worthwhile with the rest of your life. As much as I love basketball, it was merely the vehicle for achieving that higher, longer-term goal.

OPPORTUNITIES ARISE WHEN YOU PURSUE YOUR GOALS

I didn't always stay focused on my long-term goals when I was in high school. What fifteen-year-old boy doesn't get caught up in chasing girls, hanging out with friends, and just chillin'? I don't want to give the impression that my teenage years were overwrought or deadly serious. I had a lot of fun at St. Joe's once I became comfortable in the classroom and on the court. I made some great friends there, but it took me a while to get accustomed to the strange ways of suburban white kids. I'll never forget the first high school party I went to as a freshman with my friends Anthony Young and Tyrone Brewer. We were the only black kids there, and none of us had ever seen a party like this. We were used to our own neighborhood parties, where there was always a lot of loud music and wild dancing with people grooving to the tunes. This party was for the guys from St. Joseph's and the girls from a nearby all-girls school. Before we got there, we were all excited because we thought it would be like the parties we were used to. We'd even worked on some new dance moves to show off. But when we got there, we were surprised that there was no music playing. Not even a radio. There was a keg of beer, and that seemed to be the main entertainment. But we didn't drink, so we just stood around with our hands in our pockets, wondering when they were going to turn on the tunes and start dancing so we could turn it loose.

It didn't happen. They never played any music. We waited and waited. We kept thinking that maybe a deejay was going to show up. But all they did was drink and drink and drink and talk and talk. We left thinking, "Damn, what kind of party was that?"

It was a different world, and eventually I learned to adjust to it. I knew I came from a poor family, but I guess I didn't truly understand how poor we were until I saw how most of my classmates lived—and they weren't the richest kids by any means. They were mostly just middle-class white kids. At that age, the inequity struck me as awfully unfair. I didn't resent them, but I resented a society in which so many people had to struggle just to stay alive while others appeared to have so many more opportunities.

One thing that has never left me since high school is the notion that I want to make the world better for people who have not had so many opportunities. I'd grown up hustling for money and food, so I did have a deeply rooted sense of justice— and injustice. My brothers and sisters talked a lot about the daily injustices they witnessed. Our nightly discussions rarely failed to touch on racism and discrimination witnessed firsthand.

I'll never forget being interviewed by a television sports broadcaster who asked me what I'd be doing if I weren't playing professional basketball. I told him that hopefully I would have earned a law degree and maybe won a seat in the U.S. Senate. The reporter, or maybe it was another one on the same show, made fun of that. He said something like, "What makes you think you could be a senator?" That smacked of elitism to me. Because I'm an athlete, I'm not capable of going through law school or serving in Congress? I earned my college degree the hard way, and I'm certainly more capable of representing the interests of a constituency than most sports broadcasters. It had long been a goal of mine to be in a position to help the people who are usually forgotten or almost always misunderstood. I carried that goal into college with the full intention of following through on it, but as sometimes happens when you are pursuing a goal, a greater opportunity arose.

The dawn of the NCCA's "hardship option" made it possible for college players to enter the pro ranks early if they could prove a pressing financial need. If anyone had a legitimate claim to a hardship, I guess I did. If my most important goal was to help my family and others in need, then the hardship option provided me with a shortcut to do that. My mother had worked all of her life to support her family as best she could. She paid a heavy price. Her health was not good at that point, and while I was living comfortably at college, she was still struggling back on the West Side. That bothered me a lot, particularly when we'd go on road trips to places like Hawaii and Florida, where we stayed in nice hotels, ate at great restaurants, and enjoyed luxuries that I'd never before experienced.

After winning the NCAA championship in my sophomore year at IU, the opportunity to turn professional was even more appealing. Other players of my age, including Ralph Sampson, Dominique Wilkins, and Mark Aguirre, were being offered as much as a million a year to leave school and play in the NBA. Mark and I had talked about buying homes for our mothers as soon as we turned pro. We were eager to give them financial security and other things that they had never known. I felt that a permanent home would relieve a lot of the stress on Dear. I owed it to her.

In my first two years, I'd helped Coach Knight win two Big Ten titles and the NCAA championship, so I felt I'd more than paid back my scholarship. Indiana officials would have liked me to stay to help them win more championships, but I had a deeper obligation to my mother. The choice was really pretty simple. I checked my roots and took measure of my life up to that point. Those who had been there for me, who loved me, protected me, and sacrificed to bring out the best in me, were in need. I was in a position to help them and to make their lives better, just as they had done for me. At the same time, I wasn't abandoning my goals or my principles in leaving school. I could continue with my studies in the off-season and work toward my other long-range goal of getting a law degree and working within the system to help others.

When I thoughtfully measured at the roots of my goals, it seemed almost selfish to continue on in school for another two years. Going to class, studying, and playing basketball was a lot of work. It's not as glamorous as it looks from the outside, believe me. But it was also exciting and joyful to play the game that I loved at such a high level of competition, with so many fans sharing in our successes. There was still a pureness to college basketball that you just don't get in the pros. In the final evaluation, it was more fun than work, more pampered than hardship, and I could not shake the feeling that the time had come to pay back the people who had supported me throughout my life and made my success possible.

There were no guarantees that I would succeed at the professional level. More than a few commentators and even some people within the league expressed doubts because of my age— I was only nineteen when I left IU—and my height. No one questioned my heart or my dedication. But I guess they liked what they saw. The Dallas Mavericks had the first pick in the draft in 1981. They had talked about taking me, but they took Mark instead. The next team, the Detroit Pistons, took me as the second player in the draft. Mark and I each signed to play for $400,000 a year, and our signing bonuses brought the total to more than $1 million.

I have to admit that my first big expenditure was not a house for my mother—that was the second thing I bought. It wasn't a sports car or a mansion for myself, either. Instead, I got my first haircut at a real barbershop. That was a big luxury for me. I'd never had a barbershop haircut before. My mother or sister had always done it. So, it was a real luxury for me to have a professional cut my hair, and then to reach into my pocket and pay him the cash. Next, I bought Dear a house in the suburbs, where she could be safe. At first, she tried to talk me out of it. She said I didn't owe her anything, but I owe her everything. It was fitting that on Mother's Day in 1987, she attended the graduation ceremonies and accepted my bachelor's degree at Indiana University. I wasn't there. I was with the Pistons in a play-off game against the Atlanta Hawks. It was a good day in a number of ways because while my mother was tearfully accepting my college degree, I was making the last-second shot that beat the

Hawks in the play-offs. If you measure at the root, there was a certain symmetry to it, don't you think?

FUNDAMENTAL POINTS

- Goals are your stepping-stones. They determine the course you follow in your personal life, your work or career, and in your relationships with others.
- Imagine yourself at different points in the future—five, ten, twenty, thirty, and forty years down the road. Think of where you'd like to be and what you'd like to be doing at each point in your life, and then set your goals accordingly.
- Write down your goals and keep them where you can refer to them often. By having them in mind at all times, your goals will translate into actions and accomplishments.
- By setting goals and constantly working toward them in spite of distractions and frustrations, your life will pick up positive momentum.

3.

GO DEEP FOR COMMITMENT

I was twelve years old and shining shoes for meal money in Red's Pool Hall when Forte charged in with two of his boys. I heard the door fly open and I sensed his rage before I felt the sting of the gun barrel against the back of my head. Then I heard Forte bark: "Don't nobody move!"

He was looking for the punk who had just raped his little sister. It wasn't me, of course, but at that point it didn't matter. Forte was ready to kill anyone. Kneeling there with a gun barrel to my head, I lost control of my body. Everything in me poured onto the bare wood floor. Don't ever let anyone tell you that won't happen. When there's a gun at your temple, it happens.

Many times in my boyhood, I had to make instantaneous judgments that were truly life-or-death decisions. Most days, I'd step out the front door and into a war zone. Was the gangbanger on the corner two blocks down looking for a victim, a woman, a drug score, or a dice game? Was the car moving along the sidewalk a plainclothes cop, a guy looking for drugs, or a drive-by shooter? You develop keen instincts in a neighborhood where life and death are part of the day to day. This was one of the scariest situations I'd ever faced. Did Forte—whom I'd known most of my life, who was a friend of my brothers—did he really mean to kill me? Or did he simply want me to not move like he'd said? *Should I run, or should I stay still?* In flashes, I saw myself trying to sprint out the door just a few feet away. I was fast but not as fast as a finger on a trigger, or a bullet. The good guy doesn't always get away in the real world. I'd already been to the funerals of guys who hadn't dodged the bullets. And so, I fought back my instincts to run. I stayed there with the gun to my head.

Forte sounded deadly serious, but he wasn't focused on me. I was just the guy closest to the door. He knew I hadn't messed with his sister. He was looking for somebody else. His boys found the guy they were looking for at the back of the pool hall. It was another kid from the neighborhood. I knew him. We'd walked into Red's together that day. He was dragged out alone. They took him into the alley and beat him until they thought he was dead. Many years later, Lord Henry told me that after he heard about Forte putting a gun to my head, he'd taken measures to make certain that Forte realized his mistake. He never bothered me again.

A LIFE COMMITTED TO SUCCESS

Growing up on the West Side either destroyed you or fortified you for a life's worth of challenges. I survived. My experiences there and the memories I formed are part of me. I don't recommend the ghetto life to anyone. There was one West Side gang that left a nickel on the forehead of any rival gang members it killed. The message was that if you defied this gang, your life wasn't worth a plug nickel to them. Can you imagine growing up under that sort of pressure? I wouldn't want my own children to grow up threatened by daily violence or gnawed at by hunger pangs every night. Yet, I probably would not have had the sustained success that I've had in my life if it weren't for aspects of my character forged on those streets. What didn't kill me made me stronger; whenever I've faced a challenge since then, I've been able to draw strength from the fact that what I dealt with and survived as a boy was far more challenging.

Once you have identified long-term goals based on your dreams for a better life, you should commit to doing whatever it takes—mentally, physically, and emotionally—to achieve them. Commitment powers dreams and goals into reality. It is the engine that moves the wheels. Without commitment, you go nowhere. People who never commit fully to their goals often feel lost or stuck. They are out of gas. They blame their "stuck" circumstances for their misery instead of taking responsibility for their own happiness and success. Their lack of commitment is a result of their lack of inner motivation.

With commitment, you can change not only your life but the world around you. Those whom we honor and remember the most are generally those who have committed their lives to bettering the world and then lived that commitment. The Reverend Martin Luther King Jr. once said: "I won't have the fine and luxurious things of life to leave behind. . . . I just want to leave a committed life behind."

You are fully committed to your goals when you decide that nothing will throw you off course in your pursuit of them. Not racism. Not threats of violence. Not despair. Not discouragement. Not the doubts or disparaging words of other people. When you commit to your goals, you develop the attitude that no one can stop you. No one can make you give up. Simply "trying" isn't enough. When you get married and you are asked, "Do you take this person to be your lawful wedded spouse?" The right answer isn't *I'll give it a try*. It's *I do*. Nike didn't build a successful company around the slogan "Just try." It's *Just do it!* That shows an all-out commitment.

A coach once gave me a great example of what that means. We were having a breakfast conversation about the varying levels of dedication shown by players around the league. The coach looked at his bacon and eggs and then noted that some guys gave to their teams only as much as the chicken had given to our meals, while others brought more to the table. "Sure, the chicken made a contribution to this breakfast by laying the eggs," he said, "but the pig that was butchered for the bacon, it made a real commitment!"

I'm not saying you have to be willing to be slaughtered to prove your commitment to your goals, but you may well have to push yourself beyond any point you've ever gone before. You may have to go deep into your most powerful sources of determination and strength so you can go for your goals as if your life depended upon them. I've had a lot of kids tell me, "I want to play in the NBA someday." When I hear them put it that way, I'm usually skeptical, so I ask them what they've done to commit themselves to achieving that goal. Often, they'll look at me in confusion, so I'll ask them questions. Do they play ball every day? Do they practice dribbling and shooting with both hands? Do they eat well and work on strength and agility? Do they watch college and professional games to see what it takes to play at that level? Do they study hard so they will be eligible to play? Usually, they admit that they have not put that much effort into it. I can tell if someone is far more committed if they say, "I'm *going* to play in the NBA someday." There is a much greater sense of commitment apparent in those words.

THE STRENGTH OF COMMITMENT

Did you ever wonder what a basketball player thinks when he stands at the free throw line with the score tied at the end of a game and thousands of opposing fans waving signs and screaming at him to throw up a brick? In high school, college, and even the pros, I'd think of that day in Red's Pool Hall. Then, I'd get a smile on my face as I looked at all those crazy people in the stands trying to throw me off my game, and I'd think: *Do you really think you can intimidate me? After what I've seen and done in my life? It's not going to happen here, folks. Say good night, because this game is over!*

Sure, I was frightened when Forte put the gun to my head. But I didn't lose control of my mind. I weighed the circumstances and, under threat of death, I made the right decision. Had I bolted, Forte, in his rage over the rape of his sister, might well have killed me just to make a point. That was the nature of life and death on the West Side. It might have destroyed me. It destroyed many people around me. Thankfully, I survived and it made me stronger.

When I'm faced with everyday challenges, particularly those that don't involve a loaded gun, I welcome them. That moment in Red's Pool Hall was one of the most terrifying encounters of my life—and one of the most useful memories in my memory bank. When I was playing, I thought of it at least once in every game. It is a tool I use to make myself stronger in times when I feel I'm being tested. It was an ugly incident and tragic for most of those involved. Yet, it is part of where I came from and part of who I am.

I wouldn't want to go through anything like that ever again, but I've called upon the memory of it many times as a way to steel myself for other challenges. In critical moments, I go inside to a solitary place in my consciousness. In a sense, I go deep to make a withdrawal from a "strongbox"—the vault of memories and experiences that I use as sources of inner strength and motivation. Over the years, it's become a form of meditation for me. It's almost a spiritual thing. At first, I did it unconsciously, but now it is a very conscious process. I become focused on the challenge at hand, then I connect where I have been (my past experiences) to where I want to go (my goals). I think about the things I've seen and gone through—things that challenged me but eventually made me stronger. I also consider certain things my mother and other family members have done that inspire me and encourage me. It's amazing how the simple act of going deep into the well of my past can lift me up and give me strength to move forward.

I did it many times as a player in basketball games when I was under pressure to take a key shot, trigger a big play, or shut down a tough opponent. If I felt the pressure getting to me, I'd keep from panicking by going deep inside myself for a split second on the floor or during a time-out. I'd call up that memory from Red's Pool Hall and I'd think, *I was strong then—as a boy with a gun to my head—I can be strong now.*

As an athlete, I became convinced that I could beat a basketball opponent because I felt I had deeper reservoirs of strength and commitment than anyone else. If an opposing player dove for a ball, I dove with him, only harder. If one of the other team's players came barreling down the lane, I'd step up and take him down, or get taken down. I believed I could outplay my basketball opponents because I felt I'd been through more than they had and that I was willing to go further to win than they were.

I didn't know the entire life histories of each and every guy I played against, of course. Some of them probably had been through hardships too. Some undoubtedly felt just as driven as I did. Yet, I'd tell myself that no one had deeper reservoirs of inner strength to tap than me. If I felt my own strength depleting, I had only to think about my mother and the steel in her backbone. I'd reflect on how much she had sacrificed, how hard she had worked and fought for us, and I could feel the blood pump faster from my heart, strengthening my arms and legs, and my will to win. Sometimes I got a little carried away. I once bit Robert Parrish of the Boston Celtics while fighting him for the ball. Another time, I slapped Rick Mahorn of the old Washington Bullets for setting a hard pick on me. Those guys were twice my size, but I was blinded by my determination and inner drive.

I was confident that I could handle Michael, Magic, or Larry Bird one on one when the game was on the line. They were bigger and stronger, but I felt the advantage was mine because of the depth of my commitment and desire. They were great competitors, but, rightly or wrongly, I was convinced that their lives had been easier than mine. I'd already overcome such tremendous odds just in surviving the circumstances of my boyhood, I felt I had no more fears to conquer. I even took on Bill Cartwright, who was only a couple inches taller than me—if you folded him in half. It seemed like Cartwright, who is more than seven feet tall, was always taking shots at me in our playing days. He's actually not a bad guy in civilian clothes, but on the basketball court he regarded me in the same manner as a big old Clydesdale regards a horsefly. I was something to be swatted if I got too close.

In the spring of 1989, the Pistons were rolling toward our first NBA championship. But the Bulls had their own ideas. We were their toughest opponents in the division, and although we had the reputation of being bad boys, they were not exactly choirboys. We'd already played them five times earlier in the season and I had the scars to prove it. I'd come away with two cuts and a total of eleven stitches—nearly all of them courtesy of Cartwright's flying elbows.

Still, I wasn't going to back down from him or his deadly hinges. We played on April 7, and in the first quarter I stripped the ball away from big Bill, who forgot that basketball is not a contact sport. He took a roundhouse swing at me that missed, but he followed it with a punch to the back of my head. Turning the other cheek did not occur to me. I had no doubt he was intentionally trying to put a serious hurt on me. So I waded into the big octopus. I felt that Cartwright had been gunning for me for a long time and I was tired of it. I lost my temper and my senses. After all, his arms were very nearly longer than my entire body. If my manager had set up this fight, I'd have fired him. Somehow, though, I managed to land a flurry of punches to his face before my teammates Bill Laimbeer and Rick Mahorn stepped in and got me out of there before Cartwright uncorked on me.

We were both tossed out of the game and it was only then, when my heart stopped pumping, that I realized my hand was throbbing. I really think I hurt it when trying to break my fall after Cartwright's initial shot at the back of my head. At any rate, it was broken, and the doctor said I'd probably be out six to eight weeks. But I was committed to helping my teammates win the championship that year, so I convinced the doctor to put a splint, rather than a cast, on the hand, which was swollen so bad it looked like a helium-filled surgical glove. In the end, I missed only two games. It took more than a month before I could use the hand effectively, but I stayed committed to the goal, and we got it. We went on to win our first NBA championship that year.

My battles with Cartwright were rough, but it was Utah's Karl Malone, a bodybuilder moonlighting as a basketball player, who gave me what was probably the fiercest blow I ever took in a game. It was 1991 in Salt Lake City. He gave me an elbow shot to the head that knocked my lights out. When I regained consciousness they had to take me into the locker room and put forty-one stitches above my eyebrow to close the wound. And then I went back into the game to let Malone know that I'd taken his best shot and he hadn't knocked me out of the game—for more than a few minutes, anyway.

THE CONTENT OF YOUR CHARACTER

What am I made of? Have you ever asked yourself that question? What drives you? What keeps you striving? If your answer is "nothing," then you need to look deep into your heart and soul and identify your own untapped sources of inner strength and determination. They are there. Each one of us has faced challenges and persevered at some point in life. Maybe you faced a fear and overcame it. Maybe you were challenged by a bully and didn't back down. Maybe you had to run three miles in bad weather and didn't give up. You don't have to have conquered Mount Everest to build a source of inner strength. It can be any small but highly personal victory over adversity. Form a mental picture of it in your mind. See yourself putting it in a private place, your own inner sanctum, and then go there when you need to fortify your commitment and determination.

The Reverend Martin Luther King Jr. said that the ultimate measure of a man is "not where he stands in moments of comfort and convenience, but where he stands at times of challenge and controversy." Memories or thoughts that inspire, motivate, and focus you can get you through those times. By choosing to view the most challenging periods of your life as sources of strength—rather than traumatic or fearful episodes—you create a positive and goal-oriented self-image. What you achieve in life is determined largely not by what others think of you but by what you believe about yourself. Those beliefs are based on your past experiences—your successes, failures, victories, defeats, embarrassments, mistakes, and triumphs. We act according to the images we form based on those experiences. If you choose a self-image rooted in past failures or fears, then it is unlikely that you will accomplish much. If you instead build a self-image based on your accomplishments and strengths, you very likely will have a life of high achievement. The important thing to understand is that you are in control of your self-image. You can change it at any point in your life by consciously deciding to trust and believe in the best that lies within you and your life experiences.

It has always worked for me. When there are challenges in my relationships with family members, I have only to think about how hard Dear worked to keep us together and out of harm's way. Even today, when I encounter difficulties in coaching, in my business enterprises, or in my personal life, I will reflect back on how I once survived by shining shoes, begging and hunting for food on the streets. Those memories remind me of where I came from and how far I've climbed. They are the best source of strength because they are from within me.

Our characters are formed by our experiences and how we choose to respond to them. It's not something you can go to the gym or the library to develop. It comes only through facing challenges head-on and, whether you overcome them or fall short, learning from the experience and moving on. Your character can be measured not so much by how you do in your first attempt but by whether you give up or keep trying. Defeat comes only in giving up. Without an inner source of strength, you will have a difficult time overcoming all of the obstacles you will encounter as you pursue your dreams and goals. And there will be obstacles, just as there will be people who tell you that you are crazy, that you don't have a chance, and that you should just give up. There is no obstacle that you cannot get over, around, or through, and the only way you can be stopped is if you give up. By going deep, you will build the physical and mental toughness to stay on course.

GOING DEEP FOR MENTAL TOUGHNESS

The mind game is a big part of professional sports, and there are a lot of people in business who also try to get inside your head and throw you off course. I've been in business negotiations in which the people on the other side of the table have said or suggested things that seemed totally irrelevant or way off base. It confused or angered me until I realized that they were simply trying to see how committed I was to making the deal. They were hitting me with the business equivalent of an elbow shot to the ribs. Fortunately, or maybe unfortunately, I've had plenty of experience with that in sports and I was able to see it coming in business too. That's why I never get involved in a business endeavor unless I'm fully committed to it and ready to do whatever it takes to get the deal I want.

On the court, Michael Jordan was a master at the mind game as well as the physical game. He'd get inside his defender's head and then leap over his body. It's funny that he complained so much about the Pistons being a bunch of dirty players. A few years later, he didn't seem to mind playing with former Bad Boys Dennis Rodman and John Salley. Michael was as crafty at bending the rules of the game as anybody. And nobody played the referees and the crowds more skillfully.

We were wise to Michael's ways and we worked to get inside his shaved head and shake things up too. One of our favorite ploys after we'd given the Bulls a hammering was to tell reporters that the Bulls would win a lot more games if Jordan weren't such a ball hog. Michael usually scored at least thirty-five points a game, and that was if you double-teamed him. If you played him one on one he might hit fifty or sixty points. We'd always play up the fact that he'd gotten a lot of points but his team had still lost. I'd say things like, "Michael's great, but he doesn't make his teammates better and that's the measure of true greatness." That was basically a lot of B.S. because he was one of the few players who could win games all by himself. We *wanted* him to pass to his teammates because he was killing us.

Every player in the NBA tries to gain any advantage possible. It's a chess match as well as an athletic contest, and it's a great place to study human nature. Those who succeed in accomplishing their goals in sports and in life are those who are strongest mentally as well as physically. A mental letdown can be every bit as devastating as a physical one. I experienced the truth of that in the spring of 1987 in Game Five of the Eastern Conference Finals with the Boston Celtics. Up to that point in the series, we'd fought to a 2–2 game tie with the Celtics. We were hoping to go back to Detroit with a 3–2 advantage in the best of seven series, giving us a chance to clinch the series at home in Game Six.

Game Five was at Boston Gardens. It was an intense back-and-forth battle, but near the end we felt certain we were going to win it. With five seconds remaining in the game, we were up by a point, 107–106, and the Celtics had lost the ball out of bounds at our end of the floor. I stepped out of bounds on the sideline to throw it in, but the referee started his five-second, inbounds count before he even handed me the basketball. He was on a "two"-count before I touched it. I had to grab it away from him just as he counted three, and as a result I panicked, and out of fear of losing, I rushed to throw the ball in bounds to Bill Laimbeer in the low post.

I never saw Larry Bird coming. For all I knew, he dropped out of the sky. As a great player, he had instinctively sensed my panic and fear. He capitalized on it by stepping into the passing lane and grabbing the ball. For a split second, it looked like he was going to fall out of bounds with the ball, but Bird defied gravity, spun, and fired the ball to his teammate Dennis Johnson, who went in for a lay-up with one second showing on the clock. And that was it. They won 108–107. It gave the Celtics a 3–2 advantage in the series, and they went on to win it, ending our dreams of a championship for another season.

I was stunned after that game. My teammates were shocked too. It was a big letdown on my part and a brilliant steal by Bird, who had read my panic perfectly. I had played a nearly flawless game up to that point; thirty-six points, thirteen assists, and four steals. On the previous play, I'd made the shot that put us up by a point. Then, *boom*. I panicked and it was all over in an instant. I'd been with the Pistons for seven years at that point. We'd fought our way out of the league's cellar, year by year by year. I'd learned to adjust my game, cutting back on scoring and looking to set up the offense for the good of the team. I'd become its captain and floor leader in the process. Yet, I'd lost my composure at a critical point in a very important game, and I made a deadly mistake. Not only did that play cost us the game and a shot at the championship, it became one of Bird's career highlights. No player enjoys being the victim of another guy's great play. Especially one that is broadcast over and over again in highlight films. A video clip of Bird stealing my pass was still available on the NBA's Web site the last time I looked, but I don't have any bad feelings about it. Larry only did what I had done many times myself. He saw an opponent's weakness and he capitalized on it.

GOING DEEP FOR PHYSICAL STRENGTH

The most competitive athletes, like Larry Bird, have highly refined predatory instincts. They play at a heightened level of awareness and they can sense mental letdowns as well as physical weakness in an opponent. That's why I tried to never let an opponent see me rubbing or favoring an injury. If I sprained my right ankle, I'd rub my left arm. Otherwise, you could bet that someone on the other team was going to come at you to test the strength of that ankle. Some guys would do it by seeing you could go to your right or left. Other guys were less analytical and more ruthless. They'd stomp on the injury to see if you could take it.

When the Bulls beat us in the 1991 play-offs, I'd missed half the season after having surgery on my right wrist, my shooting hand. I'd just come back for the playoffs and Michael Jordan whacked that wrist at every opportunity. Bill Laimbeer did the same thing to the Celtics' Kevin McHale when he was playing on a broken foot. Laimbeer spent more time standing on Kevin's foot than Kevin did. Guys can get away with that on the court because everyone recognizes that it is part of the competition. If Michael had come up to me on the street and whacked my wrist, it would have been a different story. But in the court situation, you accept it and expect it as part of the game.

I had a reputation even in high school for being able to play in spite of injuries. I did it by going deep. In my junior year at St. Joseph's, we were 31–1 and just a couple games away from the end of our regular season when I went up for a lay-up in a game and someone undercut me. I landed awkwardly and blew out the cartilage in my knee. It hurt to even look at it. Mr. Pingatore took me to an orthopedic surgeon that night. He said the bad news was that the cartilage was totally blown. The good news was that I could keep playing because the damage was already done. I'd need surgery after the season, but if I could stand the pain, I could keep playing. Going deep got me through the pain and all the way to the final game of the 1977–78 Illinois State High School Tournament. We didn't win that game, but it wasn't because I lacked strength of commitment.

GOING DEEP TO CONQUER EMOTIONS

Many people never act on their dreams or accomplish their goals because they are afraid to fail. I used to love competing against people like that. Easy pickings. They had everything to lose and they knew it. They were afraid to fail because they didn't think they could survive it. To them, it was too painful. That's the way I felt early in my athletic career and it was something I had to overcome. I dealt with death and the threat of it on a regular basis when I was growing up. I saw too much of it. I began to equate any failure or loss with death. That didn't make me stronger. It made me weaker. It didn't make me more committed. It made me afraid. You can't let fear rule your life. It is far better to act out of strength and commitment than out of weakness and fear.

Decisions made out of fear are almost always wrong. One way I came to understand that was by observing other players and even entire teams that blew games after building up big leads. They would change their style of play—the aggressive play that had put them ahead—in the final minutes of the game because they were afraid of losing. Suddenly, they began playing tentatively and overcautiously instead of putting away their opponents. When a team did that against us, we saw their fear and gained confidence. Eventually, I realized that when I equated losing with death, it put me in the same position. It screwed me up. It made me commit to not losing instead of to winning. My fear became a bigger threat than the guys on the other team.

Finally, I realized I really had nothing to fear about losing. I went deep inside and adjusted the knobs on my attitude screen. Instead of looking at losing as death, I began looking at it as insignificant. When I felt myself tightening up at the prospect of failure, I began an inner dialogue in which I asked myself, "What is the worst that could happen if I failed?" The truth was that I wasn't going to die. What if I lost absolutely everything I'd worked for up to that point? Well, I reasoned, since I grew up with nothing, losing everything was no big deal. I came to realize that failure wasn't anything to be feared. Failure was my home turf. I started out at failure. It's like the line from the old blues song: *I've been down so long, it looks like up to me.* Since I grew up with nothing, there is no reason for me to fear losing everything. I know I can survive and fight my way back again, no matter what happens. If I go bankrupt tomorrow, I can always shine shoes for meal money. (I'm not sure how Lynn and the kids would feel about doing it, but I'd have no problem.) There is really no *better* time to strengthen your commitment than when you have failed at something. Failure is not a permanent state of being. It is just one stop on the drive to your dreams.

Those who are not afraid to commit themselves to the things they believe in often wear scars, both seen and unseen. They wear them proudly because those scars remind them of the battles they've fought and won—and even those that they've lost but not let defeat them. You can lose to anybody on any given day, but the only person who can defeat you is the one you see in the mirror. Other people may criticize you, beat you down, betray you or disappoint you, but you are never defeated until *you* give up on your dreams. The best way to prevent that from happening is to take each setback as a lesson and then re-commit to your dreams and goals.

In 1988, our Detroit Pistons team broke free of the loser's stigma and made the NBA Finals, where we faced one of the greatest teams ever to represent the L.A. Lakers. Led by Magic, James Worthy, and Kareem Abdul-Jabbar, the Lakers were Hollywood stars. We were the blue-collar guys from the Motor City. The press picked them to win easily, which was fine with me. I like being the underdog. Considering my background and my height, it's the most natural position for me. Being picked as the easy winner put all the pressure on the Lakers as far as I was concerned.

This series was memorable for many things, most of which happened during games, but at least a couple that occurred outside regulation time. The first game of that series is often remembered for something that happened before the opening tip-off. That's when Magic and I decided to show the world that real men are not afraid to express their friendship. We had been close friends since college, and we'd often talked about the fact that young guys often felt unable to express their feelings of friendship toward each other without being criticized or taunted. We both knew this series was going to be a challenge to our friendship because we are highly competitive individuals, and because Magic's coach, Pat Riley, had made it clear that he did not approve of Magic remaining friendly to me during the play-offs.

Riley's all-or-nothing attitude is that you have to hate your opponent to compete effectively against him. He wasn't about to give either of us credit for being professionals who could separate our feelings of friendship from our drive to win. So, we decided to show him and the rest of the world that men can compete against each other while still respecting and even loving each other as friends and brothers. We did it by giving each other a little peck on the cheek at the jump ball circle before every game. Neither of us had any idea what a stir it would cause. I've always done that with my brothers. We hug each other and kiss each other on the cheek every time we see each other.

I consider Magic and Mark Aguirre to be my brothers. Mark and I used to hang out with Magic when the Lakers were in the play-offs to show our support. We were there for him after he experienced one of the biggest failures of his career, when he made a huge mistake in a play-off game against Boston. He lost track of the time left in the game and dribbled out the shot clock, which cost the Lakers a win.

LOOKING BEYOND FAILURE, COMMITTING TO SUCCESS

Some sports commentators called him "Tragic Johnson" after the game. He was devastated. Mark and I tried to console him after the game but he didn't want to talk. So we all just sat in his room for the entire night, watching TV but not saying a word. Every now and then Magic would let out a big sigh, but Mark and I kept quiet. The next morning he called us both and thanked us for being there for him.

I really learned a lot about handling loss and even more about what it takes to win from Magic, so when I finally met him in the play-offs, I didn't think a handshake was enough. It's interesting that it created such a stir back then, but now you see guys doing it all the time. During the 2000 Democratic National Convention, I saw Jesse Jackson plant a kiss on a couple guys. It struck a chord and provoked some public discussion on the nature of male friendships, and that was a healthy thing.

But we didn't do it to make a statement. We did it because we care for each other as friends. It's important to let others know that our friendship has weathered a lot of changes but we are still close. Magic, Mark, and I are now all married with children and families, but we still have that bond. And it's a good thing to let other people know that we value our friendships.

Unfortunately, Magic and I had a few scrapes during that series. Coach Riley told Magic that he was going to have to prove his loyalty to his coach, his teammates, and his fans by putting them ahead of our friendship, and I'm afraid that is what happened in the series. We had a minor scuffle in the fourth quarter of Game Four at the Pontiac Silverdome. I was driving to the basket and he moved up and shoved me as I was in the air. I came down hard and bruised my tailbone. It hurt like crazy, and when I got up I shoved him. I could tell by the way he shoved me that he was buying into Riley's view of competition. That hurt me because I thought our friendship was stronger than that. A little later in the game, we tangled again. We made light of it at the time, but our relationship cooled for a while. We've been talking more in recent years. Just lately, we've even discussed forming some sort of business partnership with each other and with Mark. We've all been involved in our own ventures and our own families in the last few years, but now we're pulling back together, as lifelong friends tend to do.

The series with the Lakers may have bruised our friendship, but it made for great basketball. From a fan's point of view, it was one hell of a series. After five games, we were up 3–2 and we were feeling good about our chances to take the championship. It was a wild time for me personally. Not only were Magic and I feuding, I was also dealing with the delivery and birth of my first child. Just a few days before Game Five, Lynn had our son Joshua. My back was still very sore from getting knocked down by Magic, and I wanted to be there for Lynn and the baby, so I had a tough time keeping focused, but we did manage to win Game Five.

In Game Six, the Lakers were up by seven points at halftime, but I felt good about the way we were playing, and I was confident that we were going to win. Early in the third quarter, I scored fourteen points to get us on the right track. But then, bad luck came off the bench and tapped me on the shoulder. I had just passed off on the fast break when I stepped on Michael Cooper's foot while running down the floor. Pain shot through my ankle and I collapsed. I thought it was broken. We were only about fifteen minutes away from an NBA championship.

I was determined not to let the injury keep me out of the game. On the floor, and then as the team doctor examined my ankle, there were a million thoughts going through my head. All of the games we'd fought to win. All of the practices. All of the game films we'd watch. All of the strategy sessions. Those things flashed through my mind and I began telling myself, *Pain is only a feeling. Block it out. Block it out.*

I went deep and hit the switch on the adrenaline pump. I had come too far to reach this point. I wasn't about to sit on the sidelines and watch. Once my ankle was wrapped, I begged our trainer to tell Coach Daly that I was ready to go back in. I had to hobble onto the court, but when I got the ball, I blocked out the pain. I scored another eleven points before the third quarter ended. Later, I was informed that I'd broken an NBA Finals record by scoring twenty-five points in that period. That's what can happen when you learn to tap your deepest reservoirs of strength in times of challenge. But this was real life, not *Hoosiers.* We came up short in the fourth quarter. After leading by three with a minute left, the Lakers scored twice, and we were unable to answer either time. The final score was 103–102. I had forty-three points at the end of the night, but it wasn't enough.

After the game, my ankle swelled up to the size of a basketball. We were playing in L.A., and the only help the Lakers offered was a bucket of ice. Fortunately, bad boys stick together. The Raiders, who had moved to L.A. at that point, offered the full service of their trainers and facilities and they tried every remedy they knew to alleviate the swelling and pain. I played in Game Seven of the 1988 NBA championship series, but I was ineffective. Rick Mahorn was also hurt and unable to play up to his usual standards. For the second year in a row, we came up short. I was determined to use the loss as a motivation rather than as a frustration, so after the game, Bill Laimbeer and I went into the Lakers locker room. We watched them celebrate and we congratulated them. Then we swiped a bottle of their champagne, went back to our locker room, and tasted it while we bawled our eyes out about getting whupped. We wanted to know what it tasted like to be the champions. And once we got a taste of it, we weren't about to give up. It was disappointing, but it wasn't defeating. Twice we'd made it to the NBA Finals and twice we battled our opponents all the way, through seven games. We'd gone from being pushovers to being warriors. In losing, we learned what it would take to win and we became even more deeply committed to doing it.

To this day a game with the Lakers gets my competitive juices flowing like nothing else. I'm coaching from the bench for the Indiana Pacers now, but when I see the Lakers on the court with my guys, I want to suit up and join the battle. They've got a great organization and I respect a lot of their people, but I want to beat them anywhere, anytime, in every way possible. It's personal. Sure, the Pistons beat them in the 1989 championship, but my goal is to beat them every time. And I say that with a smile, so you'd better watch out!

GOING DEEP GIVES YOU THE CONFIDENCE TO SMILE AND ENJOY THE RIDE

It's become something of a cliché for writers to make reference to my smile as some sort of mask for an inner ruthlessness. Not long ago a writer from a men's magazine went a little overboard. In a four-page story, he mentioned my smile *fourteen* times. He variously described it as a "sourceless, curious smile," "a smile of cold fire," and "a smile that rarely made it all the way to [my] eyes." At one point in the story, my smile was "charged by something fierce and implacable." At another, it was "bright and easy," and, later, "bright and cold."

The enthusiastic smile analyst piled it on, claiming that my grin had "a dangerous charge" that reflected my "hunger and ambition, calculation and design." Other writers have described me as some sort of "smiling assassin." It's enough to make a guy want to have his jaws wired shut. What's behind this fixation with my facial expression? And why are so many of the things they say unflattering? People are always writing that Magic Johnson's smile "lights up a room." Why do they write that my smile lights up a stick of dynamite instead?

It's all pretty silly and I try to take it in stride, but I do object to insinuations that I'm the sort of guy who would smile at you while picking your pocket, or worse. There are people who've claimed that I'm calculating or ruthless and that simply is not true. I'm a normal-sized guy who succeeded in a big man's game. When I beat those big guys, most of them, quite naturally, didn't like it. You aren't much of a competitor if you enjoy getting beat. And most people don't have anything nice to say about the guy who just whupped them, especially if he is half their size. I'm not ruthless. I'm competitive. I had to outthink, outhustle, and outplay guys who were bigger and stronger than me. Some of them tried to hurt me, and I wasn't going to let that happen if I could help it. I don't expect them to like it if I beat them, and some of them I beat pretty regularly. I believe in treating people fairly, according to the rules of the game. I have the same approach to business. I'm fair with those who are fair with me. If someone tries to take advantage of me, I'm going to do my best to make sure that doesn't happen. But I don't think I've ever intentionally done anything that was ruthless or underhanded. I've been successful in sports and business because the people I work with trust and respect me.

Like Magic, I smiled a lot on the basketball court for the simple reason that I was genuinely enjoying myself. I was playing a game that I loved. I was happy when they handed me the ball. I was happy when I got to shoot and even happier when the darn thing went in. I was jubilant when we won but even when we were losing, I loved being wrapped up in the game that has been my refuge, my outlet, and in many ways my salvation. My tendency to enjoy myself during even intense competition sparked a lot of the conjecture about why I was always smiling. Maybe it's the contrast they see in a guy who naturally has a smile on his face but is also willing to play hard and to defend himself. Just because I'm competitive when I'm playing doesn't mean I'm not a good person on or off the court. Sure, I got in my share of scrapes as a player, but as one of the smaller guys on the floor, I had to make it clear that I could not be intimidated by anyone—including Bill Cartwright, whose elbows always seemed to draw a bead on my face. Bigger guys were always testing the depth of my commitment to winning, and I have the scars and crooked fingers to prove it.

I'll concede that perhaps there is something deeper than merely the joy of a moment in my smile. For a kid who took his meals where he could find them and dodged beatings and bullets on a regular basis, I've had an incredibly charmed life with a great family. I've been a champion at both the college and professional levels of sport. I've also had considerable financial and business success. What lurks behind the mysterious smile of Isiah Thomas? I submit that it's very simple. I'm very happy with my life and I'm not afraid to face anything that is thrown at me. I can smile in the face of adversity because I am confident in who I am. I can smile at people who might betray me or break their promises because I am certain that I will always find a way to succeed. I can smile at people who openly disparage me because I am confident that no matter what happens *to* me at any point in the rest of my life, *I* will determine how it affects me.

FUNDAMENTAL POINTS

- Once you have identified long-term goals based on your dreams for a better life, you must commit to doing whatever it takes—mentally, physically and emotionally—to achieve them.

- Form a mental picture of a time or situation in which you never gave up, a time when you faced your fears and defeated them, or think of someone whose strength inspires you. Store that image in your mind and use it as an inner source of strength when you need to fortify your commitment and determination to achieve your goals and live your dreams.

- Decisions made out of fear are almost always wrong. You can't let fear rule your life. It is far better to act out of strength and commitment than out of weakness and fear.

- Reject self-satisfaction, but trust in the self-confidence that comes with inner strength and a fearless commitment to your goals.

- Smile, it will make people wonder what you are up to.

4.

LEARN FROM THE BEST

There were no corporate CEOs living on the streets where I grew up. No doctors. No lawyers. No certified public accountants. No U.S. senators or Academy Award–winning directors. Standard-issue role models were in short supply on the West Side. They usually are in places where the day-to-day goal is mere survival. As a result, my early role models were not your usual white-collar professionals, titans of industry, civic leaders, or sports heroes. The leading figures in my daily life were my mother, my brothers and sisters, and more than a few unlikely role models from the streets of the West Side. They included gang leaders, dope dealers, and even the neighborhood's most notorious pimp, Don "Magic" Juan, who eventually found religion, started his own church, wrote a book, and went on *Oprah*.

None of these folks were to be found in *Who's Who* or the social register, but most were successful by our neighborhood's standards. They weren't in jail (then). They weren't panhandling. Most importantly, they were alive and thriving in an environment that was a hothouse for hostility. I learned what I could from the "best" in each of them. Author James Baldwin, who grew up in poverty as one of nine children in a Harlem family, wrote that "heroes can be found less in large things than in small ones, less in public than in private." He understood that there is something to admire and learn from in nearly everyone.

At every stage in life, it is important to identify role models—or maybe "success models"—and learn from the best they have to offer you. I've done it almost instinctively throughout my life, probably because I was the youngest in a big family, so I naturally always felt like I had a lot to learn from those around me. In preparing this chapter on role models, I thought back to the many men and women who have served in that capacity for me—whether they knew it or not—and it dawned on me that I really went to school on some of them. In certain cases, I did a lot more than simply observe these individuals. I found out what books and poems they liked and I read them. I talked to other people who'd known and worked with them. I did everything I could think of to find out what had made them successful. And in many, many ways, I reaped huge benefits from doing that.

Few things are as important as having "success" role models and mentors early on. Yet, it is a cruel fact of life that for the young people who need them the most, good role models are in short supply. While desegregation was intended to improve the quality of life for African-Americans—and in many ways, it has—some aspects of the black culture have suffered. I'm not calling for a return to the days of the "Whites Only" lunch counter, but I wouldn't mind going back to a time when even the poorest black child lived on the same street as black grocers, black clothing-store owners, black city council members, and black bankers. It's ironic that in the days of segregation blacks often lived together and nurtured each other far more than they do today. Back then, black children lived side by side with solid role models and willing mentors of their own race. Today, the neediest kids often have to select and follow their role models from afar, from television or the news media. That doesn't serve them, or society, very well. Far too many young people never develop their talents or reach their potential because they have no one to show them the way. Social workers undoubtedly would have considered me an "at-risk" kid, but I was fortunate to have a big and tight family backing me up.

A lot of the kids I knew had it far worse than I did. So many of them could have made meaningful contributions to this world if only they'd had someone who reached out at some critical point. So much potential went to waste because there was no one there to show them a way, lend them a hand, or give them hope. That's why I'm active in the 2000 for 2000 mentoring initiative in the state of Michigan. It is a program that recruits and trains mentors for kids from the age of seven to seventeen. All of the young people in the program are considered "at-risk" because each of them has faced charges for truancy or some other nonviolent, minor offense. Law-enforcement officials in Michigan believe that if these young people can get some positive guidance at this point in their lives, their chances of avoiding further problems with the law are greatly enhanced. We've lost far too many kids already, simply because they saw no way out of their challenging circumstances. Punishing juvenile offenders doesn't do any good if they aren't provided with guidance and opportunities to turn their lives around. This program, which supplements and supports other mentoring groups such as Big Brothers Big Sisters and the Boys and Girls Clubs, is built upon research that shows that mentoring can have a tremendous influence on children's lives. Public/Private Ventures, a national research organization, has found that young people who are mentored are:

- 46 percent less likely to begin using illegal drugs
- 27 percent less likely to begin using alcohol
- 52 percent less likely to skip school
- 37 percent less likely to skip a class

SELECTIVE SHOPPING IN THE ROLE-MODEL MARKET

But where do you find mentors and role models these days? The young people who need them the most are often those living in ghetto neighborhoods. Unless they have access to programs like 2000 for 2000, they don't have any way to hook up with the obvious, positive role-model choices. My advice to young people is to learn from the best within everyone they meet. I learned early in life that you can't demand perfection, even from people you look up to. That's asking for disappointment no matter where you are or how high up the social ladder you climb. Instead, I believe in buying into what is best about each person and learning from him or her. Accept that no one is perfect, but look for the good in everyone and focus on it. It's a more realistic way to live than to demand that your role models be perfect people. Even our most celebrated leaders and heroes are flawed, but their strengths have usually prevailed over their weaknesses. Sometimes they rise above their flaws over the course of a lifetime, but more often they do so for only a very few critical periods.

The Reverend Martin Luther King Jr. was a little-known minister who rose to greatness when he refused to bow to racial injustice. There are a lot of things to admire about Dr. King, but I guess what I admire the most was his courage in standing up for what he believed in, even when others—including those within his inner circle—attacked him, doubted him, or criticized his methods. He advocated nonviolent confrontation even when racists were beating and abusing him and his followers, and even when some on his side wanted to fight back with violence. He was committed to his beliefs and prepared to die for them, and that gave him the freedom to act without fear—and to change the world in the process.

On the night before he was assassinated, Dr. King told a

group of workers in Memphis, "Like anybody, I would like to live a long life. Longevity has its place. But I'm not concerned about that now. I just want to do God's will. And He's allowed me to go up to the mountain. And I've looked over, and I've seen the promised land. I may not get there with you, but I want you to know tonight that we as a people will get to the promised land. . . . So I'm happy tonight. I'm not worried about anything. I'm not fearing any man."

Nelson Mandela followed a similar path with equally powerful results. Mandela's strength of will and commitment was so powerful that even his white jailers came to believe in the justness of his cause. What could be more powerful than that? His greatest enemies, those who imprisoned him for more than twenty-seven years, eventually came to see his greatness and the undeniable truth of his belief in equality. Once again, it was his unwavering commitment to justice and nonviolence that resulted in him being released from prison and elected president of his nation. "I have fought against white domination, and I have fought against black domination," he said. "I have cherished the ideal of a democratic and free society in which all persons will live together in harmony and with equal opportunities. It is an ideal that I hope to live for and achieve. But, if needs be, it is an ideal for which I am prepared to die."

One of my biggest boyhood—and lifetime—heroes was Muhammad Ali. He was not a perfect man, by any means, but he showed me and millions of others that we can control our destinies. Dr. King, Mandela, and Ali weren't my everyday heroes. They weren't close by to show me how to survive in the day-to-day grind of the ghetto. Given that my neighborhood had far more sinners than saints, I had to become a selective shopper in the role-model market. Some of my tarnished boyhood role models may have had rap sheets instead of résumés, but there were still worthwhile things to be learned from them. Later in life, as I went through high school, college, and the pros, I had more access to role models and mentors, but many of them had their dark sides too. I learned to take the good with the bad and to learn from both.

STEALING THE BEST MOVES

I first picked up on the concept of taking the best that others have to offer while playing basketball. As a kid, and even in college and the pros, I'd watch other players and learn new moves or strategies from them. I don't think I ever played in a game where I didn't learn something from another player. Sometimes I learned it the hard way when a guy burned me with a great move or set me up.

I never "practiced" basketball. If someone had told me to go practice for a couple hours I would have told them to take a flying leap. Whenever there was a ball and a basket, I played to win, not to practice, and I played to improve my game. One of the many lessons I learned is that while other players have different levels of skill, most everyone brings something to a team. There are spot shooters and spark plugs. There are rebounders and play makers, defenders and clutch players. The best teams I've played on and against over the years are those in which every individual is valued for the role that he plays and the contributions he makes to the team effort.

Whether we were playing on asphalt or in our living room with a coat-hanger hoop, my brothers were my first heroes and role models. They were all great athletes. Most of them could have played in the NBA had they made better choices and caught a few more breaks early in life. While I worked to develop Lord Henry's deceptive, darting moves on the court, I also borrowed from my other brothers. Larry was more of a strategy player, a deep thinker who'd plan a move while lying in bed a full two days before he'd use it on the basketball court. Larry had patience. He'd watch and wait for just the right mix of players in just the right situation, and when it came, he'd show them something they'd never seen before. Larry taught me how to read a game and how to adjust my style according to the playing level and the emotional state of the other guys involved. He helped me see the whole court and beyond. What does that mean? It covers everything from the bounce in the ball to the dynamics within the opposing team and among my team-mates.

Early in our days together in Detroit, I noticed that on cer-tain nights, our workhorse center, Bill Laimbeer, just didn't have his usual aggressive juice. This was a guy who'd normally run through a brick wall to get a rebound, but on these off nights he could barely get through a small forward. He wasn't running as fast, shooting as well, or talking as much on the court, either. Our main Bad Boy suddenly took on the demeanor of Mr. Rogers. I didn't say anything to him about it at first. I wanted to see if there was any pattern. Without criticizing, I'd ask if there was something bothering him. He finally admitted after one particularly ragged game that he hadn't seen his wife or family for a few days and he missed them.

Sure enough, I noticed that every time Bill's wife went out of town during a home stand, his energy level would drop. So, I made the necessary adjustments, just as my brother Larry taught me. For example, whenever I learned that Laimbeer's wife was out of town, I ran the pick and roll with him differently. Nor-mally, I'd come off his pick, take two dribbles, and pass the ball as he went in for a lay-up. But on those days when he lacked the usual zip, I'd take an extra dribble to give him time to get in position off the pick and roll. I did the same thing when looking for him on the fast break. I don't know what was going on with him and his wife, but there was such a pattern that the other guys picked up on it too and we'd tease him about it. Then we would duck.

ROLE MODELS FROM THE REAL WORLD

As a kid, the concept of borrowing basketball moves had worked so well for me that I also began studying the actions and characters of the people around me. I watched what worked and what didn't work for them. I tried to learn from the best in everyone around me, including my brothers and sisters, my parents, friends, neighbors, teammates, teachers, coaches, and other advisors. The West Side was well populated with people living quiet, heroic lives. My mother was only one of scores of parents using whatever weapons they had to fend off despair while fighting for their children's futures. There weren't many saints among them, but I'll bet there is a special place in heaven for ghetto parents who push, prod, coddle, and kick their children into productive lives.

It's amazing how your outlook on life changes when you learn to appreciate and admire people for the good within them rather than getting hung up on their faults or weaknesses. My parents, my brothers and sisters, neighborhood characters, teachers, coaches, and business associates—from time to time all of them have shown me things that have helped me understand how the world works. Some of them never knew they were serving as my role models. Others stepped up to give me guidance. More than a few had to force their wisdom down my throat while I tried to scramble away. I owe them all a debt of gratitude. Let me tell you about a few of them, so that maybe you too can learn from their wisdom as well as their mistakes.

A FATHER'S COMPLEX LEGACY

I don't often talk about my father, who died of cancer a few years ago, because for anyone outside my family, he is a difficult person to understand. Some writers have vilified him. They've oversimplified and unfairly portrayed my childhood by saying that my father abandoned my family. Then they'd follow the clichéd story line that the poor black kid from the ghetto was molded into a man by white coaches who served as his father figures. The truth is far more complex.

My father was a proud and striking figure. He was an intelligent and ambitious person who became deeply discouraged late in life by racism and the lack of opportunities for men of our race. His discouragement turned to despair and, later, depression. He lost hope. Anger became his ruling emotion. It happened to a lot of black men of his generation, and it happens to many today, too. Racism destroys men—and women—as much by what it denies them as by what it metes out to them. My father was self-educated. He was disciplined, focused, and determined to be successful. He'd grown up in the South, where he experienced the worst forms of racism. Yet, he rose to become the first black supervisor at the International Harvester plant in Chicago. He became frustrated later in his career because his bosses would not promote him or pay him what they paid their other workers. Then, when a younger, less experienced white guy got a promotion that my father had applied for, he shut down. If he'd had access to a psychiatrist or a good physician, I suppose his symptoms would have been diagnosed as a nervous breakdown. He turned away from the world.

In his rage and despair, he simply blocked out everything good in his life. His wife. His children. The world around him. It is a family trait. We all tend to do it when we're under stress. We turn inward. I've seen my brothers do it. Having seen what it did to my father and my family, I don't allow myself to go there. My father never did go back to the job at International Harvester. He did some janitorial work, but mostly he sat and stared out the front window of the house. That's how he spent nearly every waking hour of every day for more than a year. His rage and disappointment over inequality and discrimination ate at him. Ultimately, it destroyed his marriage to my mother, and his life. He was not totally irresponsible. Nor was he an evil man. He moved out of our house a few years after I was born, but I didn't grow up hating him or resenting him. My father was there as a provider for many years for my brothers and sisters. Sadly, I didn't get to see much of the best of him. But, even after he moved away from us to be alone with his rage, he didn't leave the neighborhood. He still kept an eye on us. We had our moments together, and I benefited from the foundation he built for the family before he fell into despair.

When they were together, he and my mother set high standards for us. They stressed principles and values that have stayed with us and helped us survive. My brothers and sisters tell me that before I was born, my father would regularly call for them all to sit in a circle around him. Then he'd go around the circle pointing at each one of them, saying, "One of you, if not all of you, is going to be a millionaire someday." The message was that it was God's will for us to succeed. It was an expectation implanted in each and every one of my family members. He had the highest expectations for all of us. Being good in sports—even making it as a professional—wasn't enough. That was instilled in me from a very early age, and because of it, I prepared myself for life after basketball and I have reaped rewards beyond any expectations. So, although my father wasn't always physically there for me, he is still a part of me, and whatever success I have had is in part his legacy. He made a contribution to my life. I am a reflection of him, and his values and principles. Like my mother, he strongly believed that we had to take responsibility for our own successes and our own failures. He imparted that to his children in no uncertain terms. It came from the best of him, and I prefer to focus on that and to be thankful for it.

MY ROLE MODEL, MY DEAR

Without a doubt, my greatest role model and the most important figure in my life is my mother. She fascinates me. Even today, I can sit for hours and listen to her stories and insights into human nature. She has the uncanny power to bring out and focus on the best in people, even though she can intuitively detect the worst that is within them. She is the wisest, kindest, smartest, most loyal and fiercely determined person I've ever known. My father used to call her "Joe Louis" because she never backed down from a fight, and she rarely lost one.

When writers first described the perceived contrast between my easy-going demeanor and my inner determination and drive, I was surprised that they saw it in me, but I had no difficulty in figuring out the source. My mother has the same outer calm and inner resolve. She welcomed everyone—gang members, cops, hookers, pimps, and the homeless—into her home and shared with them what little she had, if she had anything at all. When kids from the neighborhood got in trouble with the law, she'd go to court or to the juvenile detention center and convince the judges to release the kids to her care. But if anyone tried to harm her children or interfere with her plans for them, she would unleash a ferocity that was respected by the city's toughest and most hardened street fighters.

I've heard strong women described as "steel magnolias"; Dear is a .357 Magnum magnolia. She can be as sweet or as tough as the situation requires. She gets tearful when she tells the story of why she left her family in Vicksburg, Mississippi, at the age of sixteen. The photographs of her at that age depict a beautiful young woman with high cheekbones, almond eyes, and a glowing confidence that both attracted and intimidated the men around her. Dear was almost too good-looking and too self-assured for the men of her era to bear. No man, black or white, was going to own her as her slave grandfather had been owned. Her beauty and her independence got her into trouble at a young age.

A CHAMPION FIGHTER

Dear is too proud and too strong-willed to be broken. I've been told of two major incidents that led to her leaving her hometown and the South. I'm sure there are probably more. In the first, a white shop clerk accused her of stealing something from a Woolworth's store. My mother, who was then just a teenager, not only denied the charge, she slapped the white woman for doubting her honesty. That was an understandable response, but it wasn't the wisest thing to do in the Deep South in those days. Her second confrontation with racism proved to be even more ominous.

There was a house on a hill in Vicksburg where the white men of the town went to have sex with young black women, most of whom were too poor and powerless to escape. One of the proprietors of that house had long been after my mother, trying to lure her from school or the sidewalks. Her refusals enraged him.

"The white guy had been after me for months, and one day he pulled up alongside me when I was walking home and told me to get in his truck. I refused, and he got out with a baseball bat and threatened to beat me if I didn't go with him," my mother recalled. "I had a crab-apple switch—a switchblade—in my pocket and when he came at me, I pulled it on him. I told him I was going to cut him up if he came a step closer. Just then a policeman, Officer Moorehead, pulled up. He told the guy to leave me alone and then he took me home in his car. He was a good man. He told my father that he should get me out of town because I had threatened that man, and because he probably wasn't going to give up on trying to get me up the hill. After that, my father called his brother in Chicago and sent me to him. I was out of town on the next thing smokin'."

It is difficult for my mother to tell me that story. She cries at the memory of being treated as property by the white man, but she told us the story to impart a lesson. If she was that strong and determined as a teenage girl, we could be too. She taught us to be compassionate but also to fight to the death for what we believe in.

THE BEST FROM COACH KNIGHT

When my mother felt she'd taught me enough, she turned me over to Bobby Knight's finishing school. In the mythical version of my life story as portrayed by many sportswriters and other armchair analysts, Coach Knight stepped in as a father figure and molded the raw ghetto recruit into a disciplined athlete and a confident man. I hate to burst any bubbles, but I was a pretty focused and disciplined athlete even before I arrived on the Indiana University campus. I knew that my family was counting on me. I wasn't about to disappoint them. Coach Knight was not my father figure, he was my coach—and, in spite of what others may say, he was a great coach, a brilliant basketball strategist, and in most ways a very good role model.

As I've noted before, the media and other people who see things only from a distance tend to paint people and events in terms of black and white because it is easier than trying to understand the far more complex reality. Coach Knight is one of the great coaches of his generation, a complicated man who defies any pat analysis. His volcanic temper and his in-your-face coaching style has been well documented in the media. I've felt the full force of his anger as well as the powerful light of his intellect. He ripped into me verbally and challenged me intellectually during my two years in his program. We butted heads a good part of the time, and I often resented his tactics back then. But if he called for my help today, I'd be on the first plane there and I know he'd do the same for me.

My experiences with the controversial coach mirror those of most others who played for him or against him. I was not as close to him as many of his players, in part because I stayed at IU only two years before turning pro. We didn't have a lot of contact in the years that followed, but what we did have was mostly cordial. I once gave a speech that was intended to be funny, but it embarrassed him and I thought he might never forgive me. But a few years later, Coach Knight did something that says a great deal about what sort of person he really is. After I'd been with the Detroit Pistons about five years, I got a little discouraged that we hadn't turned it around yet for the franchise. I thought I was doing all I could do, but we still weren't winning consistently at that point. I made the mistake of mentioning the possibility of retirement to someone and word got out that I might be quitting. Then, I got a letter from Coach Knight. It was a private note, so I won't share the specifics with you, but the things he wrote made a huge difference to me. He set me straight and put me on the road that led to two NBA championships. I'm not the only former player to get that sort of encouragement and support from Bobby Knight. That's why I stood by him when he was fired from the university. I am aware of his flaws, but I prefer to see the best in him, just as he has done for me. Though I've spent many hours with him, I don't pretend to know Coach Knight well. I do know that he is one of the people I'd want on my side whether in a brawl, in a debate, or in need of a "lifeline" as a contestant on *Who Wants to Be a Millionaire?*

Coach Knight has paid dearly for his failings, both personally and professionally. I know that he often has gone to extraordinary measures for his players and former players, and for his friends, at the expense of his own relationships and his own career. I don't think he gets nearly enough credit or thanks for the good that he has done. Most of his former players have become successful in careers outside basketball and inside it. Most give him considerable credit for helping them see beyond their own limitations. On the whole, his former players are extremely loyal to him. I send him letters thanking him all the time. I used to run and hide from his tirades, but now I call him frequently to ask his advice. He has a great mind for strategy.

When I first came under consideration for the head coaching job with the Indiana Pacers, I called him. He never offered an opinion as to whether he considered it to be a good or bad move for me, but he said if I took the job, he'd always be available to me. Often, it seems that everyone has an agenda that puts self-interest above all else. There are few people I trust to give me an honest assessment. One, of course, is my mother. Another is my wife. And Bobby Knight rounds out the team. It's great to have him as a friend and mentor because I know he's always going to tell it like he sees it.

Coach Knight is not the kind of guy who would wrap his arms around your shoulders and tell you he loves you like a son. But he had his own way of letting you know he cared about more than your vertical leap and your jump shot. It was near the start of my sophomore year that he called me into his office, looked me in the eyes, and said, "You can do a lot more for your race, but you're afraid."

I thought, *Where is this coming from? I'm an eighteen-year-old college basketball player, not Martin Luther King Jr.* I didn't understand at the time, but he was telling me that I had to accept the responsibilities of leadership. He understood that my success model at that point was still based in my childhood experiences. The pimp. The guys with the cars and the cash. He was trying to broaden my frame of reference and push me out of my comfort zone. He was preparing me for leadership both on the court and off. His way of doing that was to confront me, to attack my know-it-all attitude and show me that I didn't know squat. He wasn't being entirely altruistic. I was the best player on the team, and if I showed up for practice with a lackadaisical attitude, my teammates picked up on it. He needed me to push myself so that they'd follow that example.

Coach Knight challenged me to set higher goals for myself. If that is not the mark of someone who cares—a true mentor— then I don't know what is. I visited the IU campus many years after I'd left and worked out with his team. He started in on me the minute I stepped on the floor and he did not let up. I can't tell you what he said because I tuned it all out. I just smiled and said, "Thanks, coach."

BASKETBALL BOOT CAMP

Bobby Knight ran his teams in much the same way the U.S. Marines run their boot camps. Like a drill sergeant, he had to take a group of young recruits from different backgrounds and different parts of the country and quickly mold them into a unified team with shared goals. He worked to strip away the bad habits players had developed and then he rebuilt them as a cohesive unit so that they came to rely on each other as a team. As in the military, people reacted to Knight's boot-camp methods differently. Some rebelled against it. Others simply left for less combative environments. Some guys weren't accustomed to being challenged to push themselves beyond the limits they've established. Some had trouble being confronted verbally. It was the same old, same old for me. Coach Knight was no match for my mother.

When I was in grade school, I got caught swiping an apple at a neighborhood grocery. The woman clerk grabbed me and said she was going to call my mother. My response was, "Don't call her, call the police!" I always believe in taking the lesser of two evils. The juvenile justice system had no punishment comparable to what Dear could dish out. She was particularly fond of using the iron cord as a whip, but her tongue-lashings were more lethal. She wasn't afraid to unload on any of us, or on Bobby Knight either, even though she practically handpicked him to be my college coach.

When I was weighing scholarship offers, Indiana University was not my first choice, and it certainly was not the first choice of my brothers. I wanted to go to Notre Dame. It was the pick of most of my family members. I had even vowed to one of my favorite nuns in grade school that I'd play for "God's college." But Notre Dame's basketball coach, Digger Phelps, gave his last available scholarship to John Paxson instead of me. John later went on to play on a couple of championship teams for the Chicago Bulls, so he wasn't a terrible choice. But Digger has admitted that, in hindsight, he messed up by passing me up.

When Notre Dame failed to offer me a scholarship, I considered several other schools, including the University of Iowa and De Paul University, where Mark Aguirre and other longtime friends were headed. I was sorely tempted to go to De Paul, which is on Chicago's North Side. My brothers liked the idea of having me nearby, but one of them had played for De Paul coach Ray Meyer when he was a high school coach. Meyer was a legend in Chicago and a good man, but his was not a disciplined coaching style. My brothers feared that I was too strong-willed for Meyer. My mother decided that being around so many of my old friends might distract me from my studies.

THE HARD SELL

I was more disciplined than most athletes of my age and background, but I was still a teenager from the poor side of town and I was vulnerable to temptations. That became obvious when a certain college coach, who I will not embarrass publicly, showed up at our house with a briefcase containing fifty thousand dollars in cash.

You can't imagine what that stash of money looked like to my brothers and me. We used to walk with our eyes down, hoping to find a dime or quarter on the ground. As a recruiting ploy, it certainly got my attention. I'd be lying if I told you that I didn't want to take the money and run to the nearest Burger King. My brothers were all for it too.

Fortunately, my mother and my sister Ruby, who was like an assistant mother in the family, had more sense. I'll never forget that lecture. They double-teamed me. After they threw the moneybags coach out on the street, they sat me down and read me the riot act, interspersed with parts of the Emancipation Proclamation. My mother forcefully reminded me that her grandfather had been a slave and that her son was never going to be bought and sold like property.

My brothers are intelligent people, but they lost their way before completing their education. With my family's support and vigilance, I'd made it through high school, but they wouldn't be there every day to guide me through college, so my mother felt I needed to have a strong guardian there too.

She chose Coach Knight as her stand-in. Dear recognized that he was someone she could trust to step in and keep an eye on me. The coach knew exactly how to win her over. Say what you want about him—and most people have pretty strong opinions about Bobby Knight—there is no bull with him, whether he is recruiting you, coaching you, or giving you an opinion as a friend.

While recruiting me, Knight didn't tell me I was a superstar. He didn't pretend that he loved me. And he didn't offer to give me a car, cash, or even a starting position on his team. In fact, he made it clear that I'd have to fight to make the starting lineup. The Hoosiers had just won the National Invitational Tournament and his two starting guards were returning seniors. "At Indiana, the best people play," Knight told me.

He did promise that if I went to my classes and did the required work, I would graduate with a degree. He also told my mother that he'd see to it that I became a man. That impressed Dear. But it didn't impress me. I felt I was already pretty much a man. I felt certain that I'd seen things, been places, and survived situations that Knight had only read about. But I signed up because it was what my mother wanted and because, deep down, it was what I knew I needed.

My brothers were harder to convince. I love them and I always will, but my brothers were hustlers back then. They let Dear talk them out of the fifty-thousand-dollar briefcase deal, but they wanted something from Knight. They figured they'd put a lot of work into developing my game and preserving my hide. But Coach Knight didn't give out any favors to players' families. They knew that other coaches often gave players extra tickets that they could give to family members or sell themselves. Some found jobs for family members. Coach Knight made it clear that he owed them nothing. That didn't endear him to my brothers, who weren't big Knight fans to begin with. When I was still trying to decide where I wanted to go to college, my brothers warred with my sister and our mother, who thought Knight would be a good mentor for me. Then they nearly came to blows with the coach himself. The confrontation took place at my house late in my senior year of high school. Bobby Knight came to make his final pitch to get me to sign my letter of intent for Indiana University. Even though he'd won over my mother and sister, he knew there was going to be resistance from my brothers, so he brought a lot of backup. His recruiting team included Quinn Buckner, another Chicago area native, who had been Knight's star guard and captain of the undefeated 1976 NCAA championship team. Buckner later went on to win both an Olympic gold medal and an NBA title. In addition, Knight brought along the six-foot, eight-inch Wayne Embry, a former NBA player who'd become the first black general manager and vice president of an NBA team. There were also a couple of Knight's assistant coaches, a doctor friend, and, for a final safety measure, my high school coach, Mr. Pingatore.

They all jammed into our living room with Knight's gang on one side and the Thomas gang on the other. From the start it looked more like a rumble than a recruiting visit. My brothers were all over Knight and he didn't back down. They fired question after question at him, demanding to know what my role was going to be, how much playing time I'd get, and where their seats would be at home games. Gay-Gay was in typical form that evening. He had particularly strong feelings about Knight's coaching methods and he let him have it with both barrels. Bobby did not back down. It got very hostile between the two of them and finally, both were up out of their chairs and standing nose to nose, screaming at each other in the middle of the room.

Knight's team and my other brothers jumped in to break it up, but there was no salvaging the purpose of the visit, at least in that environment. Coach Knight and his entourage walked out. My brothers got into an argument among themselves as the Knight team left, and they ended up brawling with each other in the front yard. Knight's group drove to St. Joseph's in suburban Westchester and gathered in Mr. Pingatore's office. They called from there and invited me, my mother, and Ruby to come meet them. They wanted to continue the discussion—without my brothers. That's where the final decision was made that I would attend Indiana University. It was a memorable night for a lot of reasons, and for everyone involved. Mr. Pingatore told me that during the events surrounding my induction into the NBA Hall of Fame in 2000, he ran into first Quinn Buckner, then Wayne Embry, and then Coach Knight. "And every one of them brought up that night when they came to recruit you with Coach Knight and all hell broke loose," he said.

THE GENERAL'S STRATEGIES

To his credit, Coach Knight didn't make any false promises then, or at any point during my recruitment. He said only that he would help me become a better basketball player, whether I thought I needed it or not. Within a fairly short time, it was obvious that even as a freshman I was looked to as a team leader. But, to mangle Shakespeare, "Uneasy lies the head that wears the crown on a Bobby Knight team." I wasn't allowed to coast for a minute in practice, because if I did, then the other guys thought they had license to do it. Coach Knight pushed and drove me because he knew it would be relatively easy for me to slide by, and because he understood that the rest of the team would go only as far as I led them. Not that they weren't great ball players themselves. You didn't make the Indiana squad unless you had the talent. But every team has a leader and Knight was willing to cast me in that role if I was willing to run through enough walls.

After my freshman year, I felt it might be helpful to get a deeper understanding of my coach, so I spent that summer playing basketball and going to school on Bobby Knight. I'd found an intriguing newspaper article in which he listed his favorite books. Most of them were on military strategy, great generals, political leaders, philosophy, and even some poetry. Given that Knight's nickname was "The General" it wasn't surprising that one of his favorite military leaders and role models was General George Patton, but he also admired the poetry of Rudyard Kipling. I went to the library and read through a lot of the books he talked about in the article because I wanted to get a better idea of how his mind worked and what influenced his thinking. I even got a copy of one of his favorite Kipling poems, which I still have hanging on a wall in my office at home. It's called "If," and while some of the language may seem out of date, I still find the message inspiring and applicable to my daily life. It encourages the reader to "keep your head when all about you are losing theirs" and to "trust yourself when all men doubt you."

In reading the poems and books that are his favorites, I began to understand my coach's philosophy. I saw that Coach Knight prepared us for games like a general prepared his soldiers for battle. He studied our opponent's strengths and weaknesses and then drilled us on how to attack. He would dissect our previous games with a team, and their games with other opponents. By the day of the game, we would have an intimate knowledge of not only how they played but how they approached games mentally. His primary strategy was to control the battlefield by denying our opponents full use of the basketball court. He wanted them restricted to maybe one quarter of the court. If they preferred to run plays on the right side, we'd try to contain them to the left side.

Most teams establish patterns on offense and defense, and Coach Knight taught us to disrupt those patterns. I learned a great deal from him and from my high school coach, Mr. Pingatore, whose philosophy and approaches to the game were very similar to Knight's. We had our disagreements about my approach to the game, but our biggest clashes were more about my approach to life off the court. Now I understand that Coach Knight was trying to reinforce the same things my parents had always stressed. He was trying to help me see that my models for my own success were too limited. I saw myself as a basketball player rather than as a leader on and off the court. I was living out of my old environment instead of growing and looking to the future.

DEAR IN THE LOCKER ROOM

When I look back at my two years at Indiana, another thing that I respect about Coach Knight and a lot of the other people at the university was their acceptance of my family. Some of my brothers behaved pretty badly when they came to campus. A couple of them were still into drugs in those days and the prospect of coming to see me play in Bloomington, Indiana, often put them on edge. The campus in the cornfields seemed like hostile territory to my brothers, who weren't real comfortable in rural areas. On more than a few occasions, my brothers came to my games and got a little out of control, yelling things at our opponents, and at Coach Knight if he got on my case during the game.

Coach Knight never had security guards clear them out, and he was always respectful to my mother, even when she bulled her way into our locker room and gave him a piece of her mind in front of the whole team. He'd been yelling at me during a home game. At some point, he got so wound up that he said something about me that set off Dear's motherly instincts. And they are some *powerful* motherly instincts.

When the team went into the locker room at the end of the game, she followed us right on in. One of the security people told her, "We don't let nobody in the locker room."

"Well, I am *somebody* and I'm going in!" Dear said and stormed past him.

She got in Knight's face with all the media there. She let him have it with both barrels and he just stood there with his arms folded, listening. When she was finished, or at least stopped for a breath, Knight asked her a question.

"You've got all these boys, right? And when you tell one of them to take the garbage out and he doesn't take it out, what do you do?"

Dear looked at him and a smile crept over her face. "Well, I get his attention by saying: *'You SOBs take out the damn garbage!'*"

To which Coach Knight replied, "Well, Mrs. Thomas, that's all I was doing."

And that ended their locker-room debate.

But it was not the last of my mother's locker-room appearances. After the 1989 all-star game in Houston, I was giving an interview to a huge group of reporters in the locker room, when I looked up and saw my mother standing in the back.

"Dear, what in the world are you doing in here?" I asked.

"Well, Junior, you knew they couldn't keep ME out of here, didn't you?" she replied.

BUSINESS ROLE MODELS WHO PLAYED FOR KEEPS

My father taught me to be self-reliant. My mother taught me courage, compassion, and perseverance. Bobby Knight taught me to always push the envelope of my self-expectations. And I learned to honor my commitments, and to never let my guard down, from some of the most unlikely characters on the streets of the West Side.

The more I've seen of the world, the more I appreciate the lessons I learned about honor and commitment as a boy. It was a rough environment in many ways, but I learned to take my values seriously because I saw what happened to those who didn't live up to their word. It's often occurred to me as an adult that the bad thing about the business world is that liars and cheats often don't pay a harsh enough price for their dishonesty. On the West Side, justice was unforgiving, swift, and generally painful. That sounds a little harsh, I know, and I'm not suggesting that we begin executing business people who promise what they can't deliver, or those who break contracts or refuse to pay what they owe. I'm just telling you that dishonesty happens more in the so-called "legitimate" business world than on the streets. The reason is simple. The penalties for lying, cheating, or failing to pay are much stiffer on the street. There, the rats get killed or driven away so that they don't keep coming back to bite you. In the business world, the rats are protected by laws, so they keep reappearing all the time to prey on their poor victims again and again.

HARD LESSONS AND CORRUPT PRACTICES

I tend to be a trusting guy, and, it's sad to report, I've sometimes been cheated, lied to, and shortchanged as a result. When it first happened to me, I was stunned. I don't think I'd ever felt so naive in my life. It happened, fittingly, my rookie year in the NBA. Getting an NBA contract was, for me, like going from zero to a hundred and fifty miles per hour on the financial track. I went from no income to the 50-percent tax bracket in the ten seconds it took to sign the dotted line. There I was, a guy who just a few years earlier had been looking for pennies on the sidewalk, suddenly under siege by MBAs wanting to give me financial advice. Tax shelters were a big deal then. Other players talked about them in the locker room and on the bus. So, when I got a call from someone who wanted to set me up with a tax shelter, I took the time to meet with him. He was very professional. He told me about all the money I could save. He made it sound like a no-brainer. He wanted me to sign up then and there, but I told him I'd have to get back to him. I called my accountant and my lawyer. I also checked in with a couple of friends in business. They all told me the same thing. The guy was trying to scam me. He'd lied to me. At first, I couldn't believe that he'd had the nerve to sit there and brazenly try and con me. My shock was due to the fact that where I came from, you didn't do business that way, because if you did, you probably wouldn't be around long—at least not as a whole person with two arms, two legs, and the standard number of fingers, toes, eyes, and ears.

While it's a good thing to trust people, it's also wise to never let your guard down. I learned that on the streets, where con artists worked everything from shell games to dice games. And I've put it into practice many times in the world of business, starting with my tenure as president of the NBA Players' Association, which began in 1988. Back then the "Players' Association" was a bit of a misleading name for an organization that, in truth, had been run by sports agents for many years—and the players paid a price for not paying enough attention.

When I became the association's president, sports agents representing NBA players were routinely taking 20 percent of their players' salaries, and, in addition, charging them 25 percent for any endorsement contracts they brought in. Most professional athletes are in the 50-percent tax bracket because of their high salaries, so by the time the agents and Uncle Sam claimed their share, the athletes were getting about thirty cents on the dollar. Fans might have wondered how a player making more than a million a year could complain about being shortchanged, but players were contract-rich and cash-poor. Keep in mind that most NBA players support an extended family that includes not only their wives and children but also their parents, grandparents, brothers, and sisters, as well as nieces and nephews. They didn't need to be paying for their agents' vacation homes in Vail too.

One of the things that the Players' Association did while I was involved in its leadership was to cut agent fees to a maximum of 4 percent. It was not popular with the agents, but the players loved it. I got thank-you calls from a lot of them. Kareem Abdul-Jabbar was one of them. Even some of the retired players such as Bill Russell contacted me to say they appreciated what I was doing. When I entered the league, it was all but impossible to negotiate a contract without an agent. I played along for my first four years, until I felt confident enough to take control. Then I ran my NBA career like any other business. Instead of giving away 20 percent of my earnings to an agent, I hired top-notch help on a contractual basis when I needed it. I hired the best available lawyers and accountants and paid them their top hourly rate. I got better service and better results at a much fairer price. Once I became head of the Players' Association, I tried to look out for the other players as carefully as I managed my own affairs. I helped establish a prepension benefit plan that would make payouts to former players until they reached full retirement age. And, after Magic Johnson revealed that he was HIV positive, I helped the wise director of the Players' Association, Charlie Grantham, establish a sensible AIDS program for our players and the NBA.

Another Charles—Charles Bennett—was also a valued teammate during my years with the Players' Association. He was not a superior ball handler but he put up some All-Star numbers with his calculator. Charles Bennett worked for the Players' Association as an accountant but he wasn't your average C.P.A. He was trained as a *forensic* accountant by his former employer, the FBI. Charles is a "dollar detective." He tracks money like a bloodhound follows a scent. During my tenure, Charlie Grantham unleashed our former G-man upon the books kept by the NBA owners—our supposed "partners" in the league— and he took a real bite out of their wallets.

Under normal circumstances, the players would never be able to look at the financial records of the privately held NBA teams. We were given access during my tenure as Players' Association president, thanks to dissension in the ranks of the NBA owners. Jerry Reinsdorf, owner of the Chicago Bulls, was involved in a lawsuit with the other NBA team owners. He'd cut a lucrative television deal for his team, and his team only, with Chicago superstation WGN, which was broadcasting the Bulls games across the country and paying a substantial fee for the rights. The other team owners claimed that under league regulations they had a legal right to a share of any television money Reinsdorf was getting. Because of their fighting, each team's finances became part of the court record in a case that went to the U.S. Supreme Court. While they were battling it out in front of the judge, Charles Bennett spent a couple days going through their accounting books.

When he finished, the Players' Association filed a thirty-three page legal complaint against the NBA and its twenty-seven teams, charging that the owners had been underreporting their income and shortchanging the players. In 1983, the players and owners had agreed to a salary cap—a maximum each team could spend on salaries—based on defined gross revenues. Under that agreement, players were to receive 53 percent of the teams' revenues in salaries and benefits. After looking at the teams' account books, we charged that the teams had failed to report more than $100 million in revenues, thereby shorting the Players' Association of our 53 percent of that. A lot of that unreported income came from revenues earned by luxury suites and skyboxes, arena signs, and play-off ticket sales.

The NBA said it was "simply an accounting dispute." They could call it whatever they liked, but as a kid, I'd seen a lot of shell games on the streets of the West Side. The NBA owners put up a fight, but about a year after we filed the federal lawsuit, a settlement was reached. It poured tens of millions back into the pockets of players and made for a sweet victory for Charles Bennett, who became the first numbers cruncher to be named the NBA's Most Valuable Accountant by *Sports Illustrated* magazine. It just goes to show you that everybody—even accountants—have something to contribute in the game of life.

FUNDAMENTAL POINTS

- Accept that no one is perfect, but look for the best in everyone and learn from what each has to offer you.
- Don't settle for just observing your role models from a distance. If they are accessible and open to you, get to know them personally and ask them for their advice. If they are not reachable, go to school on them by reading about them, or reading what they've read. In studying their successful approaches to life, you will find models for your own success.

5.

LEADERSHIP FROM THE INSIDE OUT

I was feeling pretty good after winning the MVP award in the 1986 NBA All-Star Game. It was the second time I'd won it in just four years as a pro, but this time my celebration was short-lived. Not long after the second half of the season started, we were on a bus, returning from a game, when Coach Daly called me up and asked me to sit with him.

"What's more important to you, Isiah, having fun or winning?" he asked.

I tried to finesse what was obviously a trick question. "Well, if you are winning, you're having fun, so you should be able to do both," I replied.

"Isiah, if you want to you can lead the league in scoring every year, or you can lead this team to wins. Are you a better scorer or a better leader?"

I was beginning to catch his drift.

"A leader," I said.

"Then lead us to more wins," my coach said.

From that moment, I changed my approach as a team leader and the Detroit Pistons turned a corner. Three years later, we won the first of two back-to-back NBA championships, and we did it as a team in which nearly every player was capable—and comfortable with—stepping up and taking the lead.

LEADERSHIP BEGINS WITHIN

True leadership is not about being the most aggressive or dominant person on the court or in an organization. The leader's most important job isn't to give orders or demand allegiance. The first step of true leadership is a solitary one. It involves stepping up to the mirror, looking at yourself, and asking, "How can I be better?" You are not ready for leadership until you've reached the level where your primary contribution is bringing out the best in those around you. Coach Daly reminded me of that on the bus that day.

I considered myself a leader on the team before our little talk. After all, I was the top guy in most statistical areas and I was running the offense on the floor. But Chuck wanted me to realize that there was more to leadership than that. My perspective was all wrong. I was "showing" the way, not leading the way. I was trying to lead by example, which isn't bad necessarily—it just was not effective. I was an NBA All-Star, but the Pistons were not winning consistently. I had confused being out front with being a leader. I've seen the same "I'll do it all" mentality afflict business leaders, particularly entrepreneurs who run their own companies like one-man shows. That may work in the formative years of a business, but the one-man show rarely has long-term success. A real leader learns to trust his teammates, employees, and coworkers. Sometimes, the most effective way to lead is by stepping back so that others can step up. When you consider yourself the best player on the floor—or in the office—it is difficult to share responsibility. You tend to think you can do things better than anyone else, so you should do it all. Right or wrong, I felt like I shot better, passed better, rebounded better, and defended better than anyone else on the team. And that's how I played the game.

I came to realize that my approach to winning had been

wrong. My coach, who was the real leader of the team, had shown his trust in me by including me in discussions about strategy, and the drafting or trading of other players. But I hadn't trusted my teammates. I'd set a goal of averaging at least twenty points and at least ten assists each game, because I figured if I performed at that level, we would win. Well, we'd been winning games, but not championships.

LEARNING TO TRUST AND SHARE

After Coach Daly put me on notice that my approach to the game was wrong, I began studying the playing styles of guys whose teams were consistently in the NBA Finals. I studied everything about the moves and mental games of Larry Bird, Magic Johnson, and Julius Erving (Dr. J) because they were the three players who led their teams to championships in the 1980s. I wanted to figure out what made these guys champions. They were all great players, but even more than that, their teams were champions, and that's the ultimate measure of your success as an athlete.

It's hard to relate exactly what I took from each of them individually. All three were very smart on the court. Bird, who didn't have superior physical skills, made up for it in competitive drive and an almost supernatural court sense. He never stopped coming at you and he demanded that his teammates do the same. Magic was just one of the greatest all-around players ever. He had the great physical gifts, the work ethic, and a complete understanding of the game. His particular genius was in setting up his teammates and getting the ball to them so they could play to their strengths. Julius was the prototype for my generation of players. He was a great one-on-one player who learned to play in a controlled manner that made the best use of his teammates and their skills.

Bird, Magic, and Dr. J shared their vision of the game. They played with a love for the game and all of its nuances. They played as though it was a great party and they didn't want anyone to miss out on all the fun. From them, I learned to see not just the "whole court" but the whole game and the entire season. At a more personal level, I also took a look at winning players who were built like me. They included guys such as former Boston Celtic Nate "Tiny" Archibald, who was exactly my height but skinnier, yet he was the only player to lead the NBA in points and assists in the same season. Tiny could score. He averaged thirty-four points and 11.4 assists in 1972–73. But he toned down his flashy game later in his career to better serve his teammates. When Tiny finally won an NBA championship ring in 1980–81 with the Boston Celtics, it was at the age of thirty and in the role of a highly disciplined floor leader who barely averaged in double figures. His willingness to sacrifice his points for the good of the team, which had an outstanding record of 62–20, was recognized around the league. He was named most valuable player in the NBA All-Star Game that year.

I didn't just watch game films of Tiny and other role-model players. I tried to think like them. I changed my game as a result of what I learned. I became a much more complete player, and the Pistons became a much better team. From studying Tiny Archibald and others, I came to see that a star player stands out from his teammates. A leader doesn't always stand out at all. Instead, he brings out the best in his teammates by enhancing their strengths and compensating for their weaknesses.

I adjusted my game by focusing more on creating opportunities for my teammates. I spent much more time studying their strengths and what I could do to put them in a position to use them, while also helping compensate for areas of their game that were not as strong. From that point on, my scoring and my assists dropped. Instead of standing out, I fit in. I showed that I was focused on team play, and the other guys bought into it too. As a result, the Detroit Pistons became the only team to win an NBA championship without having at least one player averaging twenty points a game. We became focused on doing everything as a team both on and off the court. Every guy on the Pistons felt like he was an important part of the team. We became a family. There was no trickery or magic to it. It was a matter of setting high standards and giving everyone a specific role. It wasn't about demanding anything of anyone, it was about giving all you had and committing fully to the team goal. My most important job was to take Coach Daly's plan for every game and then to help my teammates make it come to life on the court.

THE VALUES OF LEADERSHIP

My high school coach, Gene Pingatore, says that while I may be a natural leader I've often had to adjust my approach. As usual, he has a point. Leadership isn't like sainthood. A halo doesn't automatically come with the job title. A leader can take his followers up with him or down with him, depending on his character. Hitler was one heck of a leader. He convinced millions of people to follow him, and he took them into some very dark places. So being "a leader" isn't enough. You have to be a leader with *integrity, maturity*, and *generosity*.

• A leader shows integrity by "walking the talk." You model the behavior that you demand of those around you. You commit to the shared goals. You value the contributions of your teammates or coworkers.

• A leader shows maturity by putting self-interest on the shelf and making the group's shared goals the priority and focus of everything he or she does.

• A leader shows generosity of spirit by sharing the rewards and the glory without measuring the size of his or her own portion. When you stop worrying about whether you are going to get yours and focus instead on the shared mission of the team or organization, then you are a true and worthy leader.

LEARNING FROM THE BENCH

I had to keep relearning the fundamentals of leadership during my years as a player, because there the role of a leader depends on the circumstances, not on the individual's personality. As a kid playing at Gladys Park or on the grade school team, I was naturally focused mostly on developing my own game and reputation. By the time I got to St. Joseph's High School, I could take over most games as the dominant player on the court. But, as Mr. Pingatore quickly pointed out dominance did not constitute leadership at that level of competition.

St. Joseph's had a very strong team in my second year. Our coach moved me up from the freshman-sophomore team to the varsity, a move that he now regards as a mistake on his part. I had not learned to play under control yet. We won only fourteen games that season, and I watched a lot of them from the sideline. Mr. Pingatore is a big Italian guy who can be as tough or as sensitive as the situation demands. In this case, he took the tough-guy route. When he felt I wasn't playing team ball, he'd yank me out of the game so fast that I'd nearly come out of my shoes.

There must have been some fishermen among his ancestors, because Mr. Pingatore was fast with the hook. Sometimes he'd sit me down before he'd send in a sub. He was particularly quick to bench me when I took a long shot from the top of the key. There was no three-point line in those days and I wasn't a very good long-range shooter. There was really no reason for me to be taking those shots. Still, I had a tendency to get the in-bounds or outlet pass, dribble down the court, and fire it up from a neighboring suburb.

Mr. Pingatore was determined to cure that tendency by jerking me out of the game each time I did it. It didn't take long before he had me as conditioned as Pavlov's dog. Oh, I'd still take the shot—for a long time I couldn't help myself—but as soon as the ball left my fingertips, I'd run over to the sideline and bench myself. I'd put the ball up but I didn't even stick around to see if it went in. I just got off the court before my coach dragged me off. It was Isiah Thomas's Bench-O-Matic Basketball.

Okay, so I was a little thickheaded that season. Mr. Pingatore will tell you that I worked hard on becoming more of a team player in the summer league and that when I came back for my junior year, I had a much better grasp of what it took to win as a team player. We went all the way to the state finals that year. We were 31–1 until we lost in the state championship game.

In my senior year, there were very high expectations. Even though we didn't have as much overall talent or experience, we were ranked number one in preseason polls. I felt the pressure in our first few games. I didn't have enough confidence in my teammates at that point, and I fell back into my old pattern of trying to do it all. In our first three games, I averaged forty points a game. But we lost two of those games, so we were off to a 1–2 start. Mr. Pingatore was not at all happy with my leadership style.

"We can't win with you scoring forty points a game," he told me. "We need you to be scoring around twenty points and working to get everyone else on the team involved in the game."

Today, Mr. Pingatore, who is still coaching at St. Joseph's, says that discussion was a turning point not just in our season but in my basketball career. I averaged twenty-four points a game for the rest of the year and we didn't lose another game until the final game in the state sectional tournament. That was a heart-breaker. I fouled out when we had a one-point lead with a couple seconds left on the clock. A guy on the other team threw up a desperate shot from way out and it went in, giving them the game. We finished my final high school season with a record of 26–3. (At my induction to the NBA Hall of Fame, a reporter asked me to name the toughest loss of my basketball career, and I told him it was that high school game.)

STEPPING UP

Even though I matured a lot as a player and as a person under Mr. Pingatore's coaching, I found that I had a lot more to learn when I entered Bobby Knight's program at Indiana University. Even Mr. Pingatore says that he thinks the greatest thing I learned from Coach Knight was leadership.

But it didn't come easy. While Mr. Pingatore often gave me rides home, invited me to dinner at his house, and counseled me about my grades and my future, Coach Knight's style was less fatherly and a lot more like tough love. That describes my relationship with him in those years. There were times when we wanted to strangle each other and there were times when I wanted to put my arms around him and tell him that I loved him.

There were more of those "love him" times *after* I left Indiana than while I was there. In the summer before my freshman year in college, I had my first impulse to choke Coach Knight. I was asked to be on the U.S. basketball team in the 1979 Pan American Games in Puerto Rico. It was a wild tournament. Coach Knight wasn't happy with the way things were run. During a practice, a policeman working security confronted him. They got into it and the scuffle ended with our coach being handcuffed and taken to jail. Puerto Rican officials charged him with assault, though they later dropped everything. I got on Knight's bad side myself a couple times during the tournament for not following his game plan, though we did take home the gold. At one point when things were not going well, I called Mr. Pingatore and told him I wasn't so sure I wanted to play for Bobby Knight in college. He assured me that I'd learn more about basketball strategy from Knight than anyone else. And he was right.

I was only seventeen years old when I arrived on the IU campus. I had a lot more growing up to do. I was confident in my basketball abilities but I didn't think of myself as a leader. I was just a freshman on a veteran team. I thought I'd take my time in getting acclimated to college life, tougher classes, living away from home, and learning a new system. Coach Knight let me know right away that he wasn't a fan of gradual introductions. He preferred the total immersion method. He came after me early and often. It was his style to challenge the strongest players. He wanted to know what I was made of so that he'd know what to expect of me in game conditions. He pushed me and there were times when I pushed back. I was a challenge to him, since I'd grown up in an environment far more intimidating than anything he could manufacture on the laid-back, rural campus. Knight probably kicked me out of practice more times than he did any other guy on the team. It finally got to the point where I'd refuse to leave. I'd just go to the opposite end of the gym and shoot around until he decided that he needed me for something. I learned to let him have his say—he always wanted the last word—and to pick out the message he wanted to deliver amid the hellfire and brimstone. I felt like Moses looking for the commandments in the burning bush.

As two strong personalities, we clashed, but I respected his thoughtful and strategic approach to basketball and he respected my ability to carry it out. Our love-hate relationship may have been tumultuous and edgy, but it resulted in some very good basketball. We won the Big Ten championship in my freshman year, and we were ranked first in the country in preseason polls going into my sophomore year. We played well up until Christmas break when we went to Hawaii for a tournament. It sounds like a wonderful trip, particularly for someone who hadn't seen much of the world, but I was really, really homesick.

As beautiful as Hawaii was, I would have preferred to be back on the West Side with my family during the holidays. I felt guilty about being in such a fancy hotel, eating great food while they were living in the ghetto. It only got worse after I called home and learned that the heat had been shut off in my mother's apartment. I was also worried because Dear had suffered a heart attack earlier in the year and she hadn't recovered completely. She had always been there for me, and the thought of her being sick made *me* sick.

I wasn't the only one on the team feeling low. We were terrible in the tournament. We played well in practice but during games we just didn't connect with each other. We lost to Clemson and to the Pan-American team—not exactly basketball powerhouses at the time. Coach Knight was furious, and as the captain I was caught in the eye of Hurricane Bobby.

It was the lowest point of my college career. Knight's fury was getting to me, mostly because I was worried about things on the home front. On the drive home for our one-day Christmas holiday, I wanted to quit the team and quit school. My life seemed like a train wreck, and it got worse after Lynn dropped me off on the West Side. No one was home. There was no heat. It was so cold that I wrapped myself up in old newspapers to try and keep warm. At that point, I didn't know where any of my family had gone, and the phone had been shut off. I'd come all the way home to be even lonelier than I was at school. I thought it was one of the lowest points in my life, but then I went back to school and Coach Knight showed me how low it could really get.

I didn't find out until several years later that when we returned home, he got together with Mr. Pingatore and asked his advice on what to do. Over the years, Bobby Knight was criticized for being arrogant, but it was mainly due to the fact that he had a low tolerance for dumb or antagonistic questions from reporters. He was humble enough that he didn't mind going to a high school coach for advice when he felt his team wasn't responding to his own methods.

Mr. Pingatore and Coach Knight talked for many hours, and they concluded that our team was very talented but lacking in leadership. The juniors and seniors on the team hadn't stepped up, in part because I was captain of the team and their leader on the floor. But I hadn't stepped up as the team's overall leader because I was still deferential to the older guys. My two coaches decided it was time to change that.

When I returned to campus, Coach Knight threw the gauntlet down. It was time for me to lead, follow, or get out of the way. We had a major blow-up as soon as I reported to his office. He said the team stunk and that I stunk most of all. He threw me off the team and said I couldn't get back on until the other players voted unanimously for my return. I ignored him and showed up for practice anyway. But I came prepared to be the leader; as a result, we went on to win the NCAA championship in the spring. When the season's stats were compiled, I led the team in scoring, assists, and steals.

LEADING AT A HIGHER LEVEL

All season, there had been debate over whether I was ready to take an NCAA hardship exemption and declare my intentions to enter the NBA draft. When we won the NCAA, it got more intense. I had no doubts that I was ready. I'd promised my mother that I would get my college degree, but I had also promised myself that as soon as the opportunity presented itself, I was going to get her out of the ghetto and give her the security and comfort she'd never known. It wasn't a difficult choice, and anyone who knew my background and my motivation understood. That included Coach Knight.

I was thrilled to be the second player selected in the 1981 NBA draft. But when I took a good look at the history of the team that had picked me, I briefly thought about returning to college for another two years—and maybe sticking around for a master's degree and a PhD. Did I really want to leave a championship college team for the doormat of the NBA? One day, the Detroit Pistons would be the Bad Boys and two-time NBA champions, but at that point the franchise was just plain *bad*. In the 1980–81 season, they'd had the second-worst record in the league. The sad thing is that their 21–61 record in that season was a *big* improvement. In the 1979–80 season, the Pistons had won only sixteen out of eighty-two games. The year before that they'd won only eleven games.

I had never before played on a losing team, nor had I ever joined one with a losing *mentality*. I could see that it had infected the entire organization, from the front office to the players, the reporters covering the team, and the fans. There was no excitement or enthusiasm in the locker room, on the court, or in the stands. The Pontiac Silverdome, where the Pistons then played their home games, could seat eighty thousand people, but they'd been drawing fewer than ten thousand on most nights. A one-ring circus drew better than the Pistons. It's a challenge to join a losing team. I was in a particularly tough situation as a rookie. I wasn't a proven veteran who could walk in and command respect. I wanted to be accepted by my teammates, but I didn't want to catch the loser's virus. At that point, the Pistons were one of the league's all-time losers. In the team's twenty-four seasons as an NBA franchise, they'd only had three seasons in which they won more games than they lost. That was scary for me. I was not interested in becoming just another cog in a broken-down machine. I didn't want to play in a negative environment that might drag my game and my attitude down, so I felt it was up to me to change it by bringing a new spirit to the team.

TEAM MOTIVATION

I won't tell you that everything that has worked for me on the basketball court will always work for you in other areas of life. Sports philosophy is often applied to business, but what worked in the Silverdome won't always hold up in the office. The principles of leadership that work in business are not always the same as those that work in sports, especially when it comes to the concept of teamwork. For one thing, there is no cheering section in the workplace. Sports teams are showered in attention and glory, which motivates team members to play at high levels. Junior accountants and sales reps don't get much adulation. They have to be motivated in other ways.

When a team wins the NBA championship, everyone from the coaches down to the trainers gets a ring. The players each get an equal share of the play-off money and they divvy the spoils with others who have contributed. When a business deal succeeds, typically it's only the people at the top who reap the rewards. Three or four executives get the credit and the big bonuses. The working stiffs on the team are lucky to get an extra day of vacation. Sports teams learn to play unselfishly because the only way to win championships is to work together. Business executives often grab all they can get for themselves, leaving nothing on the table. Just look at the salaries of CEOs across corporate America. Many of them take huge bonuses each year while their employees get minimal raises. That's why I tell managers in my businesses and others that they can't expect to motivate and inspire their employees by talking about teamwork—unless they are willing to back it up by sharing the rewards with everyone involved.

There has been a great transformation in the way the business world works in recent years because of the growing use of stock options as an employee incentive. Companies that give their employees a sense of ownership and pride in accomplishment are reaping the benefits of their loyalty and creativity. For a team to succeed in business or in sports, every participant must feel a shared sense of purpose. Motivational tricks and one-time financial incentives will not work over the long term. To be a leader, you have to communicate a sense of mission to every member of your team. You have to deliver that message from the pulpit so that everyone on the team understands how he or she fits in. You have to make believers of your teammates, your managers, and employees. Whether the goal is to win an NBA championship, to dominate an industry, or to transform a bankrupt company into a thriving enterprise, it is critical that members of your team feel that they are engaged in a process that will benefit them—not just their supervisors and their organization—for the long term.

I've seen this in both sports and business. When my partners and I purchased American Speedy in 1993, it was in bankruptcy. The franchise holders were at war with the owner, his corporate officers, and each other. There was no trust. There was no shared vision. My job was to visit each franchise owner, communicate our vision for the company, and get them to buy in. I didn't try to convince them that I knew all there was to know about the printing business. I didn't know one-third of what they knew. But I did convince them that I had a great deal of experience in the benefits of working with a team to accomplish a mutually beneficial goal. I told them about my experience of joining a dispirited and fragmented Pistons team and I told them how I worked with management to transform their franchise into a winner. Today, American Speedy is known as the Allegra Network and it is one of the world's largest printing franchises, with more than four hundred centers in the United States, Canada, and the Far East. Systemwide sales are more than $200 million. The once-bankrupt company is now a thriving business with a great future and a great team spirit.

BUILDING A WINNER FROM THE INSIDE OUT

When I joined the Pistons, my goal wasn't just to put together a winning season. I wanted to help build a dynasty capable of winning championships year after year. Looking back from the perspective of a veteran player, former general manager, and now a coach, that was a pretty bold ambition for a teenager just coming into the league. It was the only way I knew how to play the game. In fact, it is the only way I've known to live. If they ever offer a college degree in the art of winning, I should be a candidate for a doctoral degree. Not because of my own win-loss record, but because I have studied winning players and teams for nearly as long as I've been able to throw a ball. I am fascinated by the histories and philosophies of winners both inside and outside of sports. I've studied individual winners, winning teams, and, particularly, winning organizations. I had wanted to know how they were created and how they maintained their positive cultures for so long. I thought I could learn things that might help the Pistons shed their loser's mentality.

I had long admired the unity and winning traditions of "dynasty" sports teams such as the Boston Celtics, the Dallas Cowboys, the New York Knicks, and the Oakland Raiders. And so, when the Detroit Pistons drafted me, I began researching what it took to turn around a team with a losing tradition. I trekked around the country, visiting with coaches, general managers, players, and others involved in my favorite sports dynasties. I also spent a lot of time in the library, reading stories and histories of the great teams, including the Green Bay Packers, the Pittsburgh Steelers, and the Raiders. I visited the Celtics and their great former coach Red Auerbach, and I talked with him for hours. I consulted with Jerry West, the great player who had become head of the Los Angeles Lakers organization and was one of the most respected executives in sports. He generously and unselfishly gave me rare insights into the workings of their organization. Both men gave me valuable guidance into what I could do to help the Pistons develop a winner's mentality.

In my research, I formed a profile of winning individuals and winning teams. I learned that while some coaches may find short-term success through intimidation and manipulation of their players, the long-term success of sports dynasties comes when the organization is devoted to bringing out the best in all of its people. You don't create lasting bonds with rah-rah speeches and slogans plastered on the locker-room walls. You build a team by getting everyone involved, from the equipment managers to the coaching staff and owner. You help every member of the organization understand how he or she contributes to the pursuit of long-term, mutually beneficial goals. You establish a shared vision and a team culture with a standard of excellence and achievement. I learned that when you set the bar high and let everyone know that they are expected to push their talents to the limit in every practice and every game, your people rise to that level of expectation.

I also found that teams with winning traditions are not necessarily those that have the most all-stars. The greatest teams to wear the uniforms of the New York Knicks and the Boston Celtics were those in which everyone on the team contributed; even the recognized stars played unselfishly. Certainly, you have to have talented players, but the most important thing is how their skills and personalities work together. A selfish superstar may build up impressive individual statistics, but it's unlikely that he'll ever wear a championship ring. For a team to jell, everyone has to accept their roles, and someone has to make sure that they stay in line.

LEADERSHIP FROM THE INSIDE OUT

As a rookie, I had no illusions that I was going to walk onto the Pistons and single-handedly win all their games for them. Fortunately, I was joined in my first pro season by two talented guys from Notre Dame; third-year pro Bill Laimbeer, and Kelly Tripuka, another rookie who'd been a first-round draft choice. Their arrival gave me some hope, but I was still worried about my own development as a player. How was I going to be a leader on the team if I couldn't lead on the basketball court? There aren't too many six-eleven, three-hundred-pound guys willing to follow the leadership of a six-one, hundred-seventy-pound guy—unless they see that he can play at their level of skill, courage, and tenacity. I had to work on myself before I could work on them. In training camp and practices, it quickly became obvious to me that my schooling had just begun as far as the pro game. Physically, I was still a boy and they were men. Even the less skilled guys on the team had professional experience that gave them an edge over a quicker but lighter and less assured rookie. I knew the fundamentals, but I didn't know all the survival tricks of the pro game, which is much more physical, faster, and intense. I had to learn how to hold, how to push, how to place your hand on the hipbone so when your opponent tries to jump he can't get off the floor . . . all the tricks of the trade.

Just a few years' experience at the professional level can make a huge difference. Veteran players have ways of turning standard basketball techniques inside out. When I first joined the Pistons, I had a particular problem guarding against a standard offensive play known as the UCLA shuffle cut. On this play, the guard passes to the forward and the center comes up and sets a high post pick on the guard's defender—me. The fundamental, or usual method, for defending against this play is for the defending guard—me—to cut around the pick on the ball side so that he's between the forward with the ball and his own guy, who is breaking toward the basket and looking for a pass. That makes sense, except that in my first practices with the Pistons, every time that I cut to the ball side, my man would dive behind the center, catch a lob pass, and dunk it on me. Every instinct that I had said it made sense to stay between my man and the ball on that play. That basic defensive rule had been drummed into me since grade school. Every coach I'd every played for would have screamed bloody murder if I'd played it any other way. But in the pros, when you jump to the ball side, your opponent is generally so athletic and quick, he can adjust by heading for the rim and taking the lob pass. So, in the pros you play it differently, or you end up as the dupe in the other guy's highlight clip. Your only hope is that your teammates will step up and help out on defense. Without them, you will be toast.

As a rookie, and even for my first two or three seasons, I should have expected to get beaten regularly by the guys who'd mastered all the tricks. The seasoned pro can tie a younger player in knots. I had this problem when I was guarded by Maurice Cheeks, even though he was one of the few guys in the league I could look directly in the eye. Mo was playing for the Philadelphia 76ers when I joined the Pistons. He'd been in the league for three or four years by that time. Later, he made the NBA's All-Defensive Team four years in a row, and with good reason. He had quick enough hands, but he had a rabbit's feet. Some guys are described as catlike. Mo was bunnylike. He drove me crazy because he didn't guard me like other guys. I'd always played against people who did the slide and shuffle with their feet. My moves were all based on getting them sliding or shuffling one way so that I could take off in the other. But Mo Cheeks didn't slide. He didn't shuffle. He hopped. During my first few years in the league, I played Elmer Fudd to his Bugs

Bunny. He had my number. I had a really difficult time beating Mo off the dribble because it was so hard to catch him out of position. Normally, you can sense when the defender has over-committed by the way his body shifts as he moves. For instance, if a guy was sliding left with me, I'd take him further left, further left; then I would do a quick crossover dribble on him and hope-fully catch him off balance so that I could blast past him. But Mo was tough to trip up. He was like the Energizer bunny. He was a hip-hop guy before anybody knew what hip-hop was. He was so fast and agile that he always seemed to be one hop ahead. I even studied him on tapes, trying to figure out his movements. To tell you the truth, I don't think I ever figured out how to get past Mo Cheeks. Fortunately, I didn't have to play every game against him, and when I did play him, I could rely on my team-mates to set picks and help me out.

STREETWISE LESSONS IN LOYALTY

I made the usual rookie mistakes in practice, and while it was obvious that I wasn't going to turn this team around on my own, I felt that I could make an impact on the Pistons' organiza-tion by working to create a sense of unity and common purpose. I knew it was possible to pull the Pistons together because I'd seen far more undisciplined and rebellious people work together as a team. They were called the Vice Lords and the Latin Kings. The gangs of my neighborhood were powerful because of their unity. Yet, their individual members were usually not the kind of people you might describe as selfless, loyal, and full of team spirit. How, then, did the gang leaders keep them united? They built a sense of shared purpose. They convinced their members that it was in their best interest to hook up. Often, the gang leaders provided their members with things that their dysfunctional families had not given them—security, protection, creature comforts, a sense of self-worth, and even a value system. True, those values are often corrupt, but the gang leaders foster incredible loyalty nonetheless. Gang members are often willing to die for each other and for the good of their group. They endure beatings and painful initiations for the right to belong. There is a lesson in the unity and loyalty of street gangs. If they can foster unity, loyalty, and teamwork among angry and undisciplined street kids, what might be accomplished by building the same shared sense of mission into a team of more positive and more disciplined athletes?

My goal with the Pistons was to build a team that considered anything short of a championship to be unacceptable. I wanted them to hunger for a championship the way I used to hunger for a decent meal. But first I had to get a taste of it myself. That's why I attended the NBA Championship Finals every year I played in the league, whether or not my own team was in contention. I wanted to see not only how the games were won but also what it sounded like, felt like, smelled and tasted like to be the championship team. I went to every game and I also finagled my way into the winner's locker room at the end of each Finals series. I was there to congratulate them, but I was also there to get my free sample. I watched Magic and his teammates whoop it up after they beat Philadelphia in 1982, and to see their joy close at hand was exhilarating and inspiring to me. I watched them pour champagne all over each other, and laugh and cry and hug their families and friends. Then, I tucked it all away in my memory bank. When I walked out of their champagne-soaked locker room, I was more determined than ever to experience for myself the elation of an NBA championship.

Over the years, I visited a lot of celebratory locker rooms inhabited by the Lakers and the Celtics, which were the power-

house teams in the early 1980s. Like the Knicks teams that dom-
inated earlier decades, these had individuals who were among
the greatest to play the game; but in each case, the stars did not
dominate so much as delegate. If you look at their statistics in
those championship seasons, you'll find that Larry Bird and
Magic Johnson put up scoring numbers that, while good, were
comparable to those of many other less celebrated players. Taken
alone, their scoring would not suggest that these two guys played
for dominant teams with outstanding records. Yet, because they
were willing to play as team members rather than stars, Larry
and Magic became champions.

That was an important lesson for me to learn, and it wasn't
an easy one. As a rookie, I set statistical goals for myself. I wanted
to average at least twenty points and ten assists per game. I had a
great rookie year by following that plan, and it helped generate
some excitement and optimism for the team. But eventually it
became clear that if the Pistons were going to become a
championship-caliber team, a certain point guard on the team
was going to have to forget about his personal stats and make
some adjustments in his game.

CREATING A POWERFUL SENSE OF IDENTITY AND SHARED PURPOSE

I learned from watching street-gang leaders in my old neighborhood that if you want to be the most powerful "team" you have
to define your identity, carve out your turf, and defend it fear-
lessly. Often, victory goes to the team that overpowers other
teams with its confidence, unity, and efficiency. In the 1980s, the
Boston Celtics team was a powerhouse with great confidence
and a powerful identity. The championship banners hanging

over the distinctive parquet floor of Boston Gardens were just part of the team's "Celtic pride" mystique, which they used to intimidate opponents. They were masters of the pregame psych-out. Bird, Kevin McHale, Robert Parish, and the other guys would never smile during warm-ups. Instead, they'd stare at the other team's players or tell them how badly they were going to beat them. One of the first things that bothered me about the Pistons when I joined the team was that they had no psychological edge. There was no sense of destiny. No proud tradition to build upon. When new players joined the Celtics, they knew that they were going to be expected to play disciplined team basketball because of their long history of playing that way and reaping the rewards. We didn't have that in Detroit and it put us at a disadvantage. When we played teams with stronger identities and winning traditions, we were intimidated. I'd seen the power of intimidation used in other arenas. Muhammad Ali's mind games sometimes defeated his opponents before he even threw a punch. He outraged some people by predicting knockouts and even naming the rounds in which they would occur. But he also let his opponents know that he did not doubt his ability to knock them unconscious.

One of my favorite football dynasties was the Oakland Raiders, with Kenny "the Snake" Stabler, Lyle Alzado, Lester Hayes, Howie Long, Ted Hendrick, and Otis Sistrunk, who was once described as looking like a football player drafted out of "the University of Mars." They were celebrated around the world as a group of fearless misfits who came together as a great, dominating team. I had the Raiders in mind when, in the late 1980s, we finally shed our doormat image and became known for our hard-nosed play. We'd grown physically stronger through the acquisition of guys like Bill Laimbeer, Dennis Rodman, and Rick Mahorn. Now when teams came at us, we didn't back down. Even Michael Jordan noticed. In our hard-nosed play-off series against the Bulls in 1988, he called us the dirtiest team in basketball. I liked that. Michael might have been trying to get the referees to watch us more closely, but he did us a favor.

THE BIRTH OF THE BAD BOYS

As a criminal justice major in college, I'd studied the sociological effects of labeling on individuals. Labels will define you unless you take control of your image. I knew that if we branded ourselves as a tough, fearless team that didn't back down or give up, it could work to our advantage just as the Raider's wild bunch image had worked for them. I suggested to the team that we adopt a line from *Scarface* in which one of my favorite actors, Al Pacino, tells a crowd in a restaurant, "Say hello to the bad guy because you'll never see another bad guy like me."

We changed the line and began using it in our pregame routine. We'd walk out and yell, "Say hello to the Bad Boys, because you ain't never going to see bad boys like us again." As the Bad Boys, we established our turf and defended it. A lot of people didn't like it, and that was understandable. At first the league itself wasn't so sure it approved. Fans in Boston and other cities began throwing beer, popcorn, and worse things at us. Apparently, they felt that bad boys deserved to be punished. We tried to show that it was all done in the spirit of competition and fun. We even cut a rap video with NBA Entertainment, Inc., and MTV that sold more than twenty thousand copies.

The old saying "nice guys finish last" has some truth in it. It's not because nice people are losers; it's because if you consistently beat everyone else, eventually you are going to make enemies. Everyone in the league respected Michael Jordan's ability to dominate a basketball game. There weren't many that would have described him as a "nice" guy on the court. He was a masterful intimidator and a serious trash talker. He just did it quietly and ruthlessly. He was brilliant at playing the nice guy in public, but Michael wasn't afraid to make enemies on the court. I understood his mentality. The Pistons were going to have to make enemies if we were going to shed our doormat image. People were used to running all over us, wiping their feet, and then slapping us on the back. I'd had enough of that. I wanted to be on the team that other guys hated to play.

The greatest benefit derived from our Bad Boys image was not so much the impact it had on our opponents as what it did for the members of our team. When I first joined the Pistons, there was no team identity other than "losers." We weren't known for being a strong defensive team, a quick team, or a high-scoring team. As a result, new players who joined the Pistons had no sense of what was expected of them. The Bad Boys identity brought a new level of intensity and a much stronger focus to our play. We went out on the court each night knowing how we were expected to play, and our opponents knew it too. When we picked up new players, they understood immediately that they were joining a team that played tough defense and took no prisoners on offense. It was no coincidence that as we began to develop our more aggressive image, we began to win more and more games. Creating the Bad Boys brand made it official. We had arrived as a team to be reckoned with, and our record reflected our unity, pride, and shared sense of mission.

LIVING UP TO LEADERSHIP'S RESPONSIBILITIES

We didn't immediately start winning every game, but as we came together as a cohesive team our record began to improve.

It also helped that the Pistons organization began adding players with skills that complemented those of myself, Vinnie Johnson, and Bill Laimbeer. With guys like Joe Dumars, Dennis Rodman, and John Salley, we were fast becoming a team with multiple weapons and a depth of leadership. The day of February 15, 1989, was a critical one in the history of the Detroit Pistons, and a real character builder for me. We were off to the best start in the history of our franchise. We had a lot of guys who could light it up offensively and we had some bruising defensive talent too. Our scoring leader was Adrian Dantley, one of the most talented athletes on our team and a very popular guy in Detroit and around the league. He was a workhorse for us, but our management and coaches had decided to take a gamble by trading him for another player who they felt might make us an even more balanced team. It was Mark Aguirre, whom everyone knew to be my best friend since grade school. I was happy to hear that we'd be playing together, but I had concerns. I knew I would take a lot of heat over the trade because everyone assumed I'd been secretly pushing for it, which was not true. I'd heard rumors that the Pistons' general manager, Jack McCloskey, one of the best minds in the game, might be trying to work a trade for Mark, but I stayed away from it because of our friendship. Mark and I had talked about it privately, but no one in the Pistons' front office approached me about it, and I didn't approach them.

In truth, it was a risky trade because we had been playing very well, and because there had been controversy surrounding Mark's performance and attitude in Dallas. He'd gotten a bad rap as a selfish player who only cared about getting his points. I knew better, but others weren't so sure. Our team had come together with a great chemistry. We complemented each other very well, and nobody wanted to see our winning ways disrupted. My teammates let me know that they would hold me responsible for my friend's behavior as a Piston. John "Spider" Salley was very clear when I ran into him on the morning that the trade was announced: "Zeke, we got your boy Aguirre, and you'd better be ready to handle it."

No pressure there. But accountability is part of the leadership package. If you are going to be out front, you have to be willing to take responsibility. As the team's captain, I expected to be held accountable. I was glad to be the type of leader that guys feel they can talk to—especially when they have concerns. I decided to try and clear the air as quickly as possible by getting Mark together with the rest of the guys so that they could let him know what was expected of him. I wanted everyone to know I put the team's goals first. At the time, it was widely known in the NBA that our team had a special plan for trying to stop Michael Jordan by double-teaming him, triple-teaming him, and sometimes having every guy on the team dogging him, if that's what it took. Our tactics became widely known as "Jordan's Rules." Very few people outside the team knew that we also established "Aguirre's Rules." When Mark joined the team prior to our next game in Sacramento, I set up a dinner for him with Rick Mahorn, Bill Laimbeer, Vinnie Johnson, and me. We were the team's veteran players and its most dominant personalities. At the meeting I laid out the rules that Mark was going to have to live by to be accepted by his teammates. Here are Aguirre's Rules:

1. You have to do what it takes to be a Piston, which means you have to play hard every minute that you are on the court.

2. You will accept the role that you are assigned for every game. There are no stars on this team. The ninth man on this team is every bit as important as you are. When we win, we are all stars.

3. If someone on the team feels you are not performing up to our standards on the court, expect to hear about it immediately, but don't take it personally.

Those were just the rules I laid out. The other guys had their own comments, and they didn't soft-pedal anything. Laimbeer, who is as blunt off court as on, gave Mark the verbal equivalent of an elbow shot to the forehead: "All the things I heard and read about you have been bad. I really don't care if they're true or not. Isiah said to give you a chance, so I'm giving you a chance."

Rick Mahorn, the master of menace, didn't soft-pedal it, either. "If you get beat by your man, don't worry, I'll be there to help. But if I get beat and you're not there to help me, that's it for you. I guarantee you I'll be hollering for Chuck to get you out of the game."

To his credit, Mark took it well. He told the guys that he had joined the team to help them win a championship and that he would do whatever they wanted him to do to make that happen. In the next few weeks, he lived up to his promise. In his first couple practices, it became obvious that he was not up to Piston standards as far as his physical condition, but he knuckled down and began running extra wind sprints and watching his diet. He also worked hard to learn our offense quickly.

It turned out to be a great trade. Mark proved to be a better post-up player than A.D. and more of an outside threat offensively. His scoring skills also drew defenders away from Bill Laimbeer, Joe Dumars, and Rick Mahorn. Nobody likes to shake up a team that is winning, but if you can add someone who is willing to fit in and play a role that strengthens the team for a championship run, it can be a great move. It certainly was in this case. With the addition of Mark, we were too deep for any other team to beat on a regular basis.

Our success that year is proof that leadership is best exercised when it is shared. When the Pistons won the NBA championship in 1989, not one of us was on the first, second, or third All-NBA team. None of us were among the league's top twenty in scoring. No one on the team averaged twenty or more points a game, or collected more than ten rebounds a game. I was ninth in the league in assists. Bill Laimbeer was ninth in rebounding. We did have two guys, Joe Dumars and Dennis Rodman, on the NBA's All-Defense team, but we had no one among the league's leaders in steals or blocked shots. We played unselfishly. Nearly every man on the team had the ability to step up and serve the leader on the court on any given night. We had great athletes who could play two or three or even four different positions, depending on what was needed against a particular opponent. It's funny, but after we won in 1989, they couldn't figure out which one of us was the team leader. They didn't know who to put on the Wheaties box. So they put six of us on it. That said it all.

FUNDAMENTAL POINTS

- Leadership is not always about giving guidance to others. Often, it is a matter of looking within and making adjustments to bring out the strengths in your teammates.
- Being a leader isn't enough. You have to be a leader of integrity, maturity, and generosity.
- Sometimes, the most effective way to lead is by stepping back so that others can step up.
- A leader brings his team together by showing each member how his or her contributions are important, and by sharing the rewards as well as the work.

6.

LIVING WITH VALUES

When I was with the Pistons we were involved in a play-off battle with a team whose star player was in the last year of his contract. It was obvious to us that he was trying to get his stats up so that he could negotiate for more money. It was also readily apparent that his teammates were mad at him because he was hogging the ball and throwing up too many shots. This was all good for us, all bad for them. When a team's value system breaks down, it becomes highly vulnerable. I can't be too specific with this story because I don't want to pick on this guy, and since I'm now back in the NBA as a coach, I'd rather not give away too much of my strategy, either.

I can tell you that we attacked this team at its weakest point—the guy who was playing for a new contract. We did it, at first, by letting him do exactly what he wanted to do on the court, for a while. We laid back and allowed him to score *a lot* of points in the first three quarters of the game. He was so focused on himself that he didn't realize what was happening to his teammates. While he fired up the ball like a human catapult, the other guys on his team stood around and watched in disgust. By the fourth quarter, the score was still close because the guy playing for himself had a lot of points. Then we shut him down. We double-teamed him so tightly that he couldn't bend over to tie his shoes, let alone take a shot.

Meanwhile, back with the rest of his team, there were a lot of cold shooters with bad attitudes. When he finally began passing off to them, they weren't involved in the game enough to make a strong effort. Half of them weren't even warmed up. Some were so ticked off at the guy that when he passed them the ball, they'd pass it back. Their attitude was, "You've been hogging the ball the whole game, don't expect us to bail you out now." We won easily that night, but it was a clear-cut case of a team beating themselves.

Sometimes you may read it in a newspaper story, but it was just as easy to read during warm-ups or in the flow of a game: A player off his game. A team coming apart at the seams. Many writers talk about sports as a metaphor for life, but the dynamics are the same. Human strengths, weaknesses, and frailties are all on full display in any game you play. And the smartest competitors learn to exploit any weakness, whether it's a player's injured left hand, trouble in his personal life, or a lack of shared values on a team of talented players.

When Phil Jackson became coach of the L.A. Lakers, they'd been knocked out of the play-offs year after year. The team's most dominant player, Shaq, couldn't seem to decide whether he was a basketball player, an actor, or a rap master. He simply didn't have his values straight. The team's other outstanding young player, Kobe Bryant, was suffering from the same symptoms. He had flashes of undeniable brilliance, but he was all over the chart. He mostly played as if he was trying to make the team instead of playing as a part of it. He and Shaq made little effort to complement each other or to help each other out. They had a load of talent but the individual players and the entire team had no shared vision or values. "I had to stop in the very first practice and tell them they couldn't work hard at a consistent energy level, they ebbed and waned. They played with intensity, without intensity. Guys couldn't hold attention. . . . I noticed the attention span would come and go. So we really had to get focused," Jackson said in a *Chicago Tribune* interview a few days after the newly focused Lakers took the 2000 NBA championship.

Injuries and mental lapses can make you vulnerable as an athlete. But in basketball, and in life, nothing sets you up for a fall like a lack of concrete values. "When a person goes against his values in the choices he makes, the failure is automatic," noted the Reverend Howard Thurman, a theologian whose writings and sermons provided the foundation for much of Martin Luther King Jr.'s philosophy. Have you ever known someone who blamed all of his or her failings or problems on other people? This sort of person is likely to say things such as: *She makes me feel so insecure. It's his fault I'm late for work. They expect too much of me.* This victim mentality is typical of a person who has never bothered to decide what values to live by. They lay blame instead of accepting responsibility. Such a person judges himself according to the values of others. That's another path to automatic failure.

THE MEASURE OF WHO YOU ARE

There is a lot of talk about personal *branding* these days. You become a "brand" in the market once you step out into the world as a person judged by what you have to offer the world—the values you represent. Like Coca-Cola, Nike, or McDonald's, your challenge is to set yourself apart from the competition by establishing a clearly defined identity. Part of this also includes establishing your values as an employee or business owner and also as an individual in every area of your life. As the Bad Boys we defined our brand. We became known as a hard-nosed group of guys who were going to go all out to win at both ends of the court. Our values were hard work, determination, courage, and competitive drive. They earned us respect among our opponents and brought us together as a team. The values that you believe in define your individual brand, which is what people measure when deciding whether or not to be your friend, hire you, or do business with you.

What exactly are values? They are proven standards, or guidelines, for living, working, and relating to other people. They shape who you are, how you live, and how you interact with others. In the art world, the term "value" applies to the amount of lightness or darkness in a painting. The quality of the values you live by affects the lightness and darkness of your life as well. Good values are those that help a society thrive. They are usually easy to identify because they have been accepted as guidelines for behavior by most major religions, cultures, and governments throughout history.

Honesty, for example, is a highly regarded value among most cultures. So is courage. So are self-reliance, loyalty, kindness, and service to others. The values that you choose to live by are personal. They may change radically as your life and circumstances change, but hopefully, you will establish a strong core of values early in life and follow them. Without certain values as guidelines, you may feel as if you are drifting along, just taking life as it comes. A strong set of values is vital to your success and to your survival in a competitive world. With them as a foundation, you can more easily act based on what you *believe in,* rather than based on what is happening to you. Values give you the power to respond to challenges thoughtfully rather than emotionally.

When you identify the values that serve as guidelines for living, you develop a sense of purpose and a clear vision of your destiny. You make important choices based on those values. *Do I go for a good time with friends, or do I stay and work a little harder? Do I spend the day at the beach, at a charitable function, or with my family? Do I spend the money on myself, or do I help out the Boys and Girls Club?* When you stick to your values, life is easier to navigate because there are guidelines in place. But when you abandon your values even momentarily, life has a way of making you pay, sooner or later. In the 1991 Eastern Conference Finals with the Chicago Bulls, I did something out of frustration and anger that I quickly came to regret. After the Bulls beat us in the final game to win that series, most of my teammates and I walked off the court before time ran out and refused to shake their hands or congratulate them.

We had a bitter rivalry with the Bulls. We'd been their nemesis for many years and there was a lot of bad blood. There were things done on both sides that were poor sportsmanship. But refusing to congratulate them was a classless thing to do, and I've always regretted it. We'd actually had the same thing done to us when we beat the Boston Celtics in an earlier play-off series, but that is no excuse. We were criticized in the media and elsewhere for doing that to the Bulls, and we deserved it. But what really hurt came much later.

A few years ago, my son, Joshua, was playing in a game for his grade school basketball team. His team lost, and he refused to line up to shake hands with their opponents. I came down from the stands and told him that he was being a bad sport. On the way home, he asked why I made him congratulate the other team: "You didn't do it when the Bulls beat the Pistons." He surprised me with that. I didn't know he was even aware of the incident with the Bulls. Kids keep you honest, and they often see and know a lot more than we give them credit for. When my son brought up the Bulls incident, I told him that I'd been wrong, and that I'd always regretted being a poor sport. I'd let my frustration and temper get the best of me, and I paid the price. I told him that I wanted him to be better than that.

As a player, as a partner, as a son or daughter, and as a father or mother, you are measured by the values that you *live by*. Not those that you simply give lip service to. If you devote yourself to excellence, community service, and reliability, that is how your brand will be known.

SHARED VALUES LEAD TO SHARED SUCCESS

Sustained motivation and focus comes only when everyone involved buys in. When an organization grows, its members can easily lose focus on its purpose and on the things that made it successful in the first place. It happened with the Pistons, and it happened with the Lakers too. It happened to IBM in the 1980s when Apple, Compaq, and others saw that businesses' needs were shifting from mainframe to personal computers. It happened to American automobile makers when they let the quality of their cars fall in comparison to those made by Japanese and European rivals.

I've been on teams in which everyone shared the same mission—winning a championship—but not the same values. It was like agreeing to get together for a picnic with a group of friends, but everyone heads off at different times in different directions. Believe me, *that*'s no picnic. Successful coaches, entrepreneurs, and other leaders win consistently because they not only communicate their values and vision but they remain focused on them day in and day out. It's one thing to stage an annual meeting full of motivational speeches and slogans plastered all over the walls. It's another thing to get everyone in the company to *live* the values set out for them.

Managers of all types have to be great communicators. They have to be vigilant about keeping the values of their organizations foremost in the minds of their employees. The Toronto Raptors were a start-up operation when I became part owner, vice president of basketball operations, and general manager in 1994. My primary mission was to establish a vision and a set of values, and then to get everyone in the organization to buy into them. We wanted patience, discipline, and growth to be the focus in the first few years of our expansion franchise. We didn't want to raise expectations too high among our fans, but we did want to give them a strong organization with hard-playing and exciting teams that they could enjoy for many years down the road. It had taken us eight years to transform the Pistons from an undisciplined, dispirited group of guys into a confident and cohesive team. I knew it would take time and a lot of work to establish that with the Raptors.

BUILDING A TEAM'S CHARACTER

It was an exciting opportunity because we were starting with a clean slate. There were no embedded hard feelings or bitter memories to deal with. It was like getting a new car without a single door ding and with an engine ready to race. My goal for the Raptors was to establish unity and a strongly defined character from the beginning, in order to build a strong foundation. We worked hard to communicate the values we felt were important for the organization and the team. Patience was a primary concern. I was not interested in going for the quick score.

I wanted to build a dynasty. Once again, I sought advice from experts. I talked to Tex Schramm, who owned the Dallas Cowboys when they were one of the most respected franchises in pro football. He gave me some interesting advice. He said that an expansion team has to look for talent in unconventional places, because it is so difficult to build a winner from rookies and cast-off veterans. When he was trying to turn the Cowboys into a winner, Tex shocked many in football's establishment in 1964 by using his ninth-round draft pick on a track star. It wasn't just any track star. It was Bob Hayes, the "World's Fastest Human."

Just prior to the draft, Hayes won two gold medals at the 1964 Summer Olympics. He tied or beat two world records. Some thought Tex was just pulling a publicity stunt when he drafted Hayes. But Schramm knew that Bob had also played a little football in college. At small Florida A&M University, Hayes had led his team to a 36–4 record during his four years on the football team, even though he had to take time off occasionally to compete in Olympic and other events as a runner.

The Dallas Cowboys never had a winning season before Bob Hayes joined the team. In his first season, he set the Cowboys' rookie receiving records with twelve touchdown catches and was selected to the Pro Bowl. The next year he was named an all-pro. After Tex Schramm drafted Bob Hayes, his team moved from the cellar of the NFL to the highest ranks. In Hayes's ten seasons with the team they made eight post season appearances, including a Super Bowl title and two NFC crowns.

Now, one man does not take a team, especially a football team, from the cellar to the penthouse. But Tex's philosophy of being willing to step outside the box and to look for talent wherever it was available helped build the Dallas Cowboys into one of football's most dominant teams. As general manager of the Toronto Raptors basketball expansion team, I set out to do much the same thing. I knew it was going to be difficult for us to build a team quickly if we relied only on the draft and the players we were given as an expansion team. So, I started looking for players in other places, including high schools. I remember that my director of scouting was not real hot on the idea. I can't really blame him. It was tough enough covering the NBA, the CBA, the European leagues, and all of the colleges. "We can't cover high school too," he told me. "The heck we can't," I responded.

My contacts in Chicago, including my brothers and sisters, had been telling me about this six-eleven kid who had transferred to Chicago's Farragut Academy high school for his senior year after being named Mr. Basketball for the state of South Carolina while playing there as a junior in 1994. When I made a trip home, I stopped by a Farragut game to see the kid play. I left after two minutes and I never scouted Kevin Garnett again. I didn't have to. I saw greatness in those two minutes and I sure as heck didn't want anyone else to know that I was interested in him. There were already reports that he intended on skipping college and going directly to the pros. I had dreams of him wearing a Raptors uniform.

I told our scouting staff to keep an eye on Garnett but to be low-key about it. But he was too good to keep a secret. There was a basketball camp for the nation's top young players in Chicago and I hoped he would skip it. He did, but he staged a private workout for any scouts who were in town. Everyone was asking me if I was going to it, but I told them I wasn't interested in seeing some high school kid work out. All the time, I was hoping he'd come down with the flu or something. As it turned out, the reports that came out of the private workout weren't all that great. Then again, maybe the other guys were playing their cards close to their chest too.

A few days before the 1995 NBA draft, my former opponent but longtime buddy Kevin McHale called me. He'd become a vice president and general manager of the Minnesota Timber-wolves NBA team. He had the fourth pick in the first round of the draft. I had the seventh. I've known Kevin since high school and I can't lie to him.

"Zeke, what do you think of this Garnett kid?" he asked.

I tried to hold back for a couple seconds, but I finally gave in. "If you don't draft him, I will," I said.

"That's all I need to know," McHale said.

Garnett made the all-star team in his second season and hasn't missed it since. Of course, *I* drafted Damon Stoudamire, who was a bit unusual as a high draft pick too, because he is only about five-ten. Then again, in his first season he was NBA Rookie of the Year! My goal was to build a young, athletic team. I focused on finding players whose skills complemented each other on court in the way that you see in great teams like the 1986 Boston Celtics, which included Larry Bird, Robert Parish, Bill Walton, Kevin McHale, Danny Ainge, Dennis Johnson, and Scott Wedman. They were the most harmonious team I've ever competed against. They played beautiful music, like a symphony or a great jazz group. They weren't just an aggressive defensive team, they were just flat-out good across the board in every area of the game. As a team, their basketball IQs were off the charts. They must have had eight guys with basketball PhDs. They'd all been well schooled in the fundamentals of passing, moving without the ball, cutting, and sharing the court. They played fundamental basketball at the highest level it can be played. That Celtics team was about as well matched and as balanced a team as you'll ever see on the court.

It was my dream to build that sort of team for the fans in Toronto. We tried to match players as teammates, rather than simply going for the all-stars. For me, a winning attitude ranked as high as a good jump shot. It was especially important to find veterans with that positive outlook, because their attitudes would influence the younger guys we were trying to bring along slowly. I knew that there would be pressures for instant results from fans and sportswriters, so I tried to communicate that philosophy throughout the team, our organization and to the media. I stressed that my primary focus as an executive was to build not just a winner but a winning tradition.

SHARED VALUES AND VISION

I knew that it would not always be easy to stand by the values I was trying to build into the organization. I expected pressure from fans who wanted a winner, and perhaps even from my co-owners who wanted to keep fans in the seats. I felt that as long as I kept reminding everyone that we were trying to build not only a winning season and a winning team but a winning tradition, I'd have no problems within the Raptors' organization.

I chose my friend Brendan Malone, a former Pistons assistant, to be the first head coach of the Toronto Raptors, because, like me, he is highly competitive and driven to succeed. Brendan is a great basketball coach. He knows the game, and he is a tireless worker who prepares for every game and expects to win each of them. In most situations with a mature team, that's a perfect philosophy. But the Raptors were an immature team. When I hired Brendan, I assured him that his performance would not be judged on how many games the team won or lost in the first year. I wanted him to focus on bringing the young players along slowly, without a lot of pressure on them, while building a strong team-oriented culture.

We were fortunate to be starting out with many talented players, including our premier first-round 1995 draft pick, Stoudamire, an all-American from the University of Arizona.

More than a few sportswriters and fans claimed that I drafted Damon because he seemed to be so much like me as a player. He is actually a few inches shorter than me, but he is also incredibly quick, unselfish, and capable of doing whatever it takes, offensively or defensively, to lead his team. Yet, he was not a popular choice with the fans, who seemed to have their hearts set on the bigger Ed O'Bannon, a six-eight forward and all-American who led UCLA to the 1995 NCAA championship.

People actually booed when it was announced that I'd picked Damon as the seventh guy taken in the first round. I was well aware that expansion teams generally try to build around a big man, but I simply felt that Damon was the better athlete and a better fit with the foundational philosophy and values I'd created for the team. As it turned out, the little guy, who wore a Mighty Mouse tattoo, made me look like a genius. He played brilliantly, leading the team in scoring, assists, and—to my chagrin—minutes played.

It became obvious early on that Damon was a dynamo, but that made me all the more concerned. I didn't want the dynamo to burn out. The NBA season is considerably longer and far more demanding than the NCAA season, with more intense competition and long stretches on the road. Many promising rookies have suffered physical injuries and mental burnout in that critical first year, because either they or their coaches push too hard upon entering the professional league. From the start of the season, I communicated to Brendan that I wanted to give Damon and the other young players time to develop. I had a five-year plan, not a one-season plan. My goal was to have everyone on the team ready, physically, mentally, and emotionally, for a championship season in our sixth year.

FAMILY VALUES

Each of us establishes our own value system. Our values change as our priorities and perspectives change. We start out, generally, with those values that our parents have lived and emphasized as we were growing up. If we're lucky, those values are worthy ones that stay with us over a lifetime. The great thing about values is that they aren't expensive. Anyone can decide to build them into his or her daily life. Rich people don't have exclusive rights to them. (You might even know of a few millionaires who don't have any at all.) My parents spent a lot of time trying to instill values in us that would help us see beyond our difficult circumstances. My father and mother particularly valued *loyalty, self-determination, compassion,* and *courage.* They preached those values to us, but, more importantly, they lived them. I wasn't around for my father's best years with the family, but my brothers and sisters and others who knew him well talk about his strength of character in those days before he fell into despair. I did witness my mother put all of these values into action in her life. She preached that your values are not something you simply wear on a button, tape on a bedroom wall, or put in a desk drawer. They are guidelines for the way you live.

There were a lot of families on the West Side with strong values. You couldn't see them displayed in a china cabinet, hanging over the fireplace, or parked in the garage, but they were there. And often, those values produced more long-term benefits than a safe packed with stocks and bonds. Hard work, courage, self-determination, unselfishness; all of these important values lived among the families on the West Side. I'm going to tell you about their impact on my family, but we didn't have exclusive rights to them. There were many, many families fighting the good fight around us. The Thomas family has received a lot of attention because of my success, but there were many mothers and fathers who struggled and strived to better their lives and those of their children. Like my brothers and sisters, there are countless other teachers, police officers, nurses, business managers, and entrepreneurs who fought their way out of poverty. Most of them did it because they established guidelines and goals that helped them focus on the possibilities and potential for their lives, rather than on challenges of their surroundings. When family members buy into shared values, there is harmony. When they don't, the family becomes fractured. I saw this when some of my brothers began to use drugs and get involved in illegal activities. It tore the family up. Fortunately, in most cases, we rallied around each other and worked to bring the wayward ones back into the fold.

LIVING WITH LOYALTY

It seemed like whenever there was a problem in our family, my mother would bring out the toothpicks. We'd each get one. Then, she'd tell us to try and break them. We did it easily, of course. Then she'd hand each of us nine toothpicks bunched together. "Now, break them."

None of us could do it.

"As long as you stay together, nobody can break you down, either," she'd say. "It doesn't mean you have to be joined at the hip, it just means you need to always be there for each other."

We were such a close family when I was a kid, I couldn't believe that brothers and sisters actually could live in different cities or states. Over the years, anytime my mother felt the family connections weren't strong, she'd bring up the toothpick lesson. It was her way of saying, "United we stand, divided we fall."

My mother was not always successful in her effort to steer us safely through the traps and snares of our impoverished surroundings. She dreamed of us all becoming doctors and lawyers. That did not happen. We've lost one brother, and from time to time others have fallen and we've done everything we could to help them get back up. Through it all, my mother has never stopped fighting for her children and believing in them. I've seen other parents give up on their children, write them off as hopeless, and walk away. Not Dear. Regardless of what we might have done, how badly we might have hurt or disappointed her, she has always been there. She has never backed away from any one of her family members. She is still there for us, and she always will be. She is as loyal and devoted a mother as anyone could want.

We've learned from her to be loyal to each other, and to those others who've earned it. Loyalty has always been important to me outside the family. It's one reason I stayed with the Pistons my entire career. When I studied other winning dynasties in sports, one of the things that stood out was the fact that most of them had players who stayed with the organization over the long term. Teammates who play together year after year learn to compensate for each other's weaknesses. They know what to expect of each other and what others expect of them. They also are not easily rattled because they can depend on each other when the chips are down.

Lord Henry went to St. Philip High School in the mid-1960s when it was still mostly a white school but slowly changing. The school had a "three-two" rule that there could never be more than three black guys playing for St. Philip on the court during a game. The team's other two players had to be white.

Lord Henry was always on the floor because he was the team's highest scorer and best player. He was doing things with the ball back then that you didn't see in the NBA until, well, until I got in the league and used what I'd learned from him. My oldest brother was a confident athlete on the basketball court, but he could be intimidated when playing in unfamiliar and hostile territory. In 1967, his senior year, they had a big game against Fenwick High School in Oak Park, an affluent western suburb where a lot of Chicago's most powerful political and business leaders lived. It wasn't far from our neighborhood, but it might as well have been another country as far as Lord Henry was concerned. We were not around white people much at all in our segregated neighborhood. And often, our experiences with them weren't the best. When I left my neighborhood and strayed into the white suburbs, I usually came home with bruises. Lord Henry had many of the same experiences. So did my mother when she was growing up in Mississippi.

Brother Alexis Kalinowski was a Servite clergyman, my first basketball coach, and the man in charge of the youth center at Our Lady of Sorrows Catholic church. He loved to tell us that when he first met my mother, he put a hand on her shoulder and she nearly jumped out of her shoes in fright. He read the fear and suspicion in her eyes and gently told her, "We need to talk. You can teach me about this community, and I'll teach you who we are." My mother often says that it was "Bro"—as everyone in the community called the priest—who taught her that not all white men are just out to use black women. He became one of her closest friends and most trusted allies—even if he did like to pull pranks on her occasionally.

When I was about eleven years old, I became very fond of Bro's dog. Since the dog was always with me, Bro finally gave him to me, but I suspect it wasn't so much an act of priestly generosity as a trick on my mother. The dog was an all-white mutt with one black spot, and he was named accordingly. The first time my mother had to stand on the corner and call for him, she got the joke. Dear heard herself yelling, "Here, Whitey! Here Whitey!" and came back laughing ruefully. "I think that damn Bro did that on purpose!" she said.

Lord Henry's concerns about playing at Fenwick were well grounded. It was a hostile territory back then, though Oak Park later became one of the more successful racially mixed communities in the country. To make my brother all the more nervous, the St. Philip fan bus broke down on the way to the game with Fenwick. So for most of the first half, the only black people in the whole gym were Lord Henry, his few black teammates, and my mother and sister, who'd come to the game with Bro. Lord Henry was a nervous wreck as the game began. The Fenwick fans were cheering wildly for their team. He couldn't dribble, pass, or shoot.

But then, just before the end of the first half, the St. Philip fan bus arrived. The doors to the gym flew open and in marched our brother Gregory, leading a big group of friends. Gay-Gay has always been the wild child of the Thomas gang. He has enough personality for an entire state. He is, as he'd say, loud and proud and ahead of the crowd. Gay-Gay was rapping before anyone knew what rap was. That afternoon, he marched into the Fenwick High School gymnasium and launched into his "Brother, I got your back" rap to let Lord Henry know that he was no longer alone.

Gay-Gay paraded through the bleachers, waving a big scarf and chanting: "Come on rat! The cat is here! I got some vodka in my lock-a. It's up on the roof, a hundred proof! We got your back, so get on the attack!"

It wasn't your typical cheer or pep talk, but then there is nothing typical about Gay-Gay. His unorthodox cheerleading did have the desired result, though. Lord Henry couldn't hit the broad side of a barn in the first half of that game. He scored forty-three in the second half. I understand now how Lord Henry felt back then. I got the same boost from seeing family members in the stands in grade school, high school, college, and the pros. Whenever it was possible, and often when it seemed impossible, they were there for me. When I say that we are a tight team, I'm including Thomas women too.

THE FAMILY TEAM

My sister Ruby was always my father's favorite child because, like him (and like our mother too), Ruby is outspoken, tough, compassionate, and extremely loyal. She's so loyal that when her first husband wanted to move out of Chicago, she told him she could never leave Dear alone. She stayed with our mother and got a new husband, Bruce Carlsen, instead. Ruby and Dear are a tough tag team and they are very protective of each other. Like the rest of us, Ruby had always gone to private Catholic schools. She was a real straight arrow who never had anything to do with gangs if she could avoid them. So she was a little shocked at the working environment on her first day as a teacher at Marshall Metropolitan High School, an inner-city school with a serious gang problem. Ruby came home in shock at what she'd seen. She told Dear she was never going back. Gang members had harassed and threatened her. They disrupted her class and ignored anything she said. It was chaos, and it was scary.

Dear wasn't very sympathetic. She told Ruby, who lives with her, that if she wanted to stay in her house, she'd better go back and take control. What my mother didn't tell her was that she put the word out on the street that the new Spanish teacher at Marshall was the daughter of Mama Thom and the sister of Lord Henry, and anybody who messed with Ruby Thomas was going to answer to them.

When Ruby returned to class the next day, she was stunned at the change. Gang members walked up to her and apologized, saying, "We didn't know you were Rat's sister and Mama

Thom's daughter." Ruby said it was actually a little embarrassing because from that point on she received a gang escort when she walked from her home to the school, and gang leaders regularly checked her classroom to make sure nobody was acting up. The other teachers suspected that Ruby had bribed or threatened someone, but it was just the power of Team Thomas in her corner.

While my family had a team mentality, we were also taught from an early age that we were responsible for our own successes and failures in life. The philosophy preached in our regular family discussion was very much one of self-determination. *Life will not hand anything to you. You have to go after what you want. Make it happen, and count on us to back you up.* My family had its challenges, but there were no "victims" living at the Thomas house. That was not part of our value system. We were taught that no one makes you give up. Only you can choose to be defeated by a situation. Life will slap you down from time to time. You will get dealt a bad hand now and then. But you are never defeated unless you give up. You cannot always control what happens *to* you, but you can choose how you respond. The most important thing is to realize that you do have a choice. Those messages of self-determination were encoded into nearly every lecture I heard growing up. My mother lectured us about it, and she lived it. She didn't sit around crying about her hardships. She either found a way or she made a way. She fought to make the best life she could for herself and her kids and it didn't end after she got us through Catholic schools. She has always let us know that we are a team, and that we can count on each other, but that we were responsible for our own successes or failures.

You don't have to look far to find victims these days. The talk shows and the newspapers are full of people blaming everyone but themselves. Yet, I've never met a victim millionaire. Or an all-star victim. Or a valedictorian victim. Why is that? It's because people who see themselves as victims rarely accomplish anything. They are too busy laying blame instead of laying bricks. They don't build, they blame. They don't create a foundation for success. They just dig themselves into a hole. The chronic victim has no dreams. No goals. No commitment. No values. No joy or gratitude.

We were taught to determine our own destinies, not to leave our lives up to other people, or circumstances, or simple luck. We were expected to swim, not to go with the tide. The value system we learned was one in which we were held responsible for our own success. No one owed us a living, happiness, love, consideration, or appreciation. We had to earn those things. That is the way life works. If you expect money, good health, respect, or love to be handed to you, your expectations are way too high. Don't feel cheated if they aren't met. You've gotten what you deserved. If, however, you commit yourself to working hard, treating people the way you want to be treated and never giving up, you will probably be rewarded in ways that you can't even dream.

LIFE—OR DEATH—VALUES

When I speak about the importance of such values to groups, particularly college students and corporate leaders, I sometimes wonder if the words ring hollow in their ears. I never wonder that when I talk to kids from the inner city. A lot of people from more affluent backgrounds become cynical about such things because they've heard so many platitudes, but often, they don't see a real commitment to values or principles like hard work, self-determination, and perseverance.

Poor kids aren't as cynical because they understand how

serious values are. If ghetto kids don't make a determined effort to develop their talents and get their educations, then they will probably never escape the ghetto. I had many lessons on the importance of self-determination. One of the wisest players that I knew in the NBA was Kareem Abdul-Jabbar, who believed that "we've got to stand by ourselves before we can make it. Nobody's going to help us."

A lot of what I learned about taking charge of my own life was drawn from the struggles I witnessed my brothers and their friends go through. I'll never forget the day Pee Wee got himself killed. It was in K-town, which is the name given to the area of the West Side along the "K" streets, such as Kedzie, Kostner, Karlov, Kedvale, and Keeler. K-town was just east of our neighborhood. It's where Mark Aguirre grew up. It was gang territory too, and Pee Wee was the leader of the ruling gang for that area, the Black Souls, which later became the Gangster Disciples.

Pee Wee was not a guy you could easily describe in black-and-white terms. He was tough and ruthless, a very shrewd leader and organizer. He was a criminal who was widely feared, for very good reasons. Yet, when he stepped outside of the gang environment, he was capable of kindness, loyalty, and many other good things. He may have busted heads on the streets, but inside the youth center where my mother worked, he always followed the rules, and enforced them too, if others didn't.

Pee Wee was extremely charismatic. He was a favorite of my mother and of Sister Kevin Ann, a nun who ran the Head Start program in our neighborhood and also worked at the youth center with my mother. Sister Kevin Ann grew up in an Irish Catholic family in Crawfordsville, Indiana. Like Brother Alexis, she became one of my mother's closest friends. She was even there when my mother gave birth to me. I've teased her that I'll never get over the fact that the first woman to see me naked was a nun!

Sister Kevin Ann (who is no longer a nun but principal of St. Patrick's School in Springfield, Illinois) remembers Pee Wee as a true gentleman—at least around her. "I never got out of a car that he didn't open the door for me if he was around," she said. "He was always doing things for me. One time, he did a little too much. I lived with a big group of nuns in an apartment building on Central Park. One morning, we all walked out to find that the batteries had been stolen out of our cars—all except mine, that is. I saw Pee Wee later that day at the youth center and I told him that while I appreciated that I had a battery that morning, the other sisters weren't real happy that mine was protected and theirs were stolen. The next morning, we found all of their batteries piled up on the front porch. Of course, the other sisters complained that Pee Wee's boys hadn't put them back in their cars."

Pee Wee was like another big brother to me, and he was a part of my family. In fact, he lived with us for more than a year after my mother bought our first house, a big wood-frame at the corner of Menard and Adams, on the edge of Columbus Park. It had been abandoned during the white flight from the West Side, but it was rehabbed under a federal program. My mother, who by then was working full-time for the city, bought it for practically nothing down, under an urban renewal program that provided low-interest housing loans.

My sister Ruby loved that big old house, which was similar to those in Oak Park. She was outraged and more than a little scared when she heard that our mother was going to rent the attic room to Pee Wee to help pay the mortgage. She cried and screamed for days. Ruby knew him only by his reputation, which was fearsome. She considered him a "degenerate" and refused to go near him. Then, one morning, he came downstairs and, before she could leave, he asked her to join him for some baked pinto beans our mother had cooked up.

They talked for hours, and Pee Wee won her over. "When you got him out of the gang, he was the nicest, kindest, and sweetest person," Ruby recalled. "When he died, I think it hurt me more than anybody."

A LIFE WITHOUT OPTIONS

I was charmed by Pee Wee too. I'd go up the stairs and visit him nearly every day, though I generally didn't say much. He was always lifting weights up there and I'd go and watch and try to lift them too. He called me "Lil' Man." As his name suggested, Pee Wee was not a big guy, but he was powerfully built and made more menacing by a huge Afro.

One day, I went upstairs and he wasn't lifting weights. He was loading a carbine rifle. "Lil' Man, this is probably the last time you'll see me again," he said. "I'm going to die today."

I didn't ask a whole lot of questions. Basically, the older guys would expect me to be quiet and listen while they imparted wisdom to me. This time, Pee Wee didn't have any trouble getting my attention. I could see that he was very serious. He wasn't playing with me.

"I'm tired of living like this," he said. "It's either going to be me or them."

Pee Wee's life had turned into a daily fight for survival with rival gang members, the police, and people seeking vengeance for something he or his gang lieutenants had done. Pee Wee had painted himself into a bloody corner. There was good in him, I'd seen it. But the good hadn't gotten him anywhere, and the bad had led to this dead end. He couldn't have been more than twenty-five or twenty-six. He'd lived a long life for a gang leader.

He told me he planned to commit a robbery at a grocery store, but it was more a suicide mission. He was dead by four that afternoon, killed by police during the robbery. He'd chosen his way out. I never even knew Pee Wee's real name. Nobody in my family did. But the message of his life was clear to me. Pee Wee was a natural leader. He could have accomplished great things. But he had no long-range focus for his life. He let his lethal environment dictate his actions. He went with the deadly flow. I learned a serious lesson from Pee Wee's death. You have to identify a way for yourself and then go after it. You can't expect anyone else to do it for you. You have to commit yourself fully to it, never give up on it.

It may seem strange that a family that was often on the run from a landlord or a bill collector would be known for providing shelter to those who had even less than they did. It may seem odd too that I often went hungry at school or at home, while my mother was feeding strays who wandered in from the streets or out of jail. I've got to admit, it seemed a little questionable to me too, back in those days. I wondered why I had to fight for a place to sleep on the floor, when some guy I didn't even know crashed on our only couch. I wondered why I got only one greasy slice of bread for dinner, yet we had enough to feed three or four stragglers off the street.

My mother lived the Golden Rule. She treated others the way she would want to be treated. Often, she knew their needs because she shared them, and if she had anything to give, it was a blessing she was willing to share. My mother understood what George Washington Carver meant when he said, "How far you go in life depends on your being tender with the young, compassionate with the aged, sympathetic with the striving, and tolerant of the weak and strong. Because someday in your life, you will have been all of these."

COURAGE IN ALL DOSES

I saved the topic of courage for last, because I doubt if it's possible to have values of any kind without it. After all, values are nothing without the courage to live them. As you realize by now, I don't have to dig deep to come up with examples for this subject. Not when there was a television movie based on my family entitled *A Mother's Courage*. If you suspected that the TV movie of our lives was not quite as gritty as the real thing, you are right. There are plenty of people, though, who will tell you that while the actress who portrayed my mother, Alfre Woodward, is a very pretty lady, the real Mary Thomas had even more going on in her day.

My mother's beauty was legendary, but her everyday bravery was way beyond that. We don't tell many of the stories about her simply because people don't believe them. They sound like urban myths. But they are all true. She was something then, just as she is something now.

Mothers in general had a special status on the West Side in those days. Gangs ran the neighborhoods, but gang leaders had mothers too. Drugs were increasingly prevalent, but this was before crack cocaine provoked so much totally senseless, random violence. Back then, unless somebody's mother wandered into the middle of a gunfight, or fell prey to a thug out of his mind from drugs or drink, she usually was given respect. My mother, Dear, had that, and power too.

She ran the Our Lady of Sorrows youth center with Brother Alexis. It was housed in the former gymnasium of what had been the Providence girls' high school. With pool tables in the basement and basketball courts upstairs, it was one of the neighborhood's few refuges from violence and gang control. Weapons were checked at the door. No hats. No fighting or cursing. Dear controlled who got in. If you ran afoul of her, you were out, and you were probably in deep trouble at home too, if you had a home.

My mother knew everyone's family down to the second cousins, and those who weren't really cousins but got called that anyway. She treated everyone equally. And if she saw someone in need, she went to Bro or Sister Kevin Ann, and they took care of that. The three of them were a sort of ruling triumvirate of the West Side, or at least in the East Garfield neighborhood that fell under the shadows of the twin towers of the basilica of Our Lady of Sorrows, at the edge of the Eisenhower Expressway near California Avenue.

Bro had a lot of clout because he started the youth center, and he coached most of the basketball teams in the parish. He was a Bobby Knight type, but with the power of God behind him. He too, was fearless. Born Theodore Kalinowski, he was orphaned at an early age. He grew up hard, moving from foster home to foster home around the West Side of Chicago, so he was no stranger to the neighborhood.

East Garfield was Vice Lords turf, but it was on the border with the Black Souls' territory. Both gangs were allowed into the youth center, but they had to leave their rivalries outside. There was rarely any serious trouble at the youth center, though their battles sometimes came onto church property. My mother and Sister Kevin Ann were working a vendor booth at the Our Lady of Sorrows annual carnival one summer night in the late 1960s when one of the forty clergymen in the parish, Brother Michael, came up in a highly agitated state. "Look up on the roofs," he said.

The carnival was in a sort of courtyard surrounded by the basilica, the rectory, and the monastery. Nearly fifty members of the Vice Lords had taken positions on top of all three buildings. They all had guns or rifles. There was no doubt about their intended targets. The Black Souls were all over the carnival.

"Get Brother Alexis," my mother told Sister Kevin Ann.

The nun found Bro and alerted him to the danger. He, in turn, went to Pee Wee, leader of the Black Souls, and together they quietly spread the word. There were more than two hundred Black Souls sprinkled in the crowd. Without looking at the Vice Lords above, Bro and Pee Wee led the Black Souls, one by one, out of the courtyard, through the rectory, and to the street, outside of rifle range. Bro then escorted them down Jackson Boulevard to Garfield Park and their own territory.

As soon as the Black Souls were out of the courtyard, my mother walked into the center of the carnival, looked up to the Vice Lords, and ripped into them. The tower spires of the basilica are probably still vibrating from the unholy hell she gave the gang members on the rooftops. With their intended targets out of range, and my mother threatening them with her eternal wrath, the Vice Lords gave it up. They climbed down without firing a single shot.

And to think, NBA fans often wondered how I could get bloodied, knocked to the floor, and stomped on in a basketball game and still get up with a smile on my face.

What was going through your head? they'd ask. *What were you smiling about?*

Now you know. It was my mother's courage.

FUNDAMENTAL POINTS

- Values are proven standards or guidelines for living, working, and relating to other people. They shape who you are, how you live, and how you interact with others.
- Strong values enable you to respond to challenges thoughtfully rather than emotionally.
- No team, organization, or enterprise can thrive over the long term without shared values.

7.

OPPORTUNITIES ARE GOLDEN

The West Side of Chicago was not widely regarded as the land of opportunity. Help-wanted signs were as rare as banks or brokerages. Storefronts were barricaded. Doors were barred. Windows were boarded up. Yet, our neighborhood was home to legions of aggressive opportunists like me and my brothers and our friends. Together and individually, we stalked the streets for opportunities. We hustled for them and chased them down. We found them in the most unlikely places and pounced on them. I was probably about ten years old when I began shining shoes with my brothers. We worked the close-in suburbs west of the city, and inside its borders near the corner of Roosevelt and Twelfth Street. Lord Henry had to be particularly careful there. He and his buddies had once worked a different game in that neighborhood. They were robbing customers as they came out of a restaurant and liquor store. They realized a little too late that some powerful people owned the place.

One night, Lord Henry, then only about twelve years old, was grabbed off a street corner by three big cops. They dragged him to an alley behind the joint. They took the grate off a sewer and lowered him headfirst into it. They held him by his legs and dangled him there while telling him what was going to happen if he and his friends didn't stop preying on the liquor store and its patrons. "They'll find you down there in the sewer eaten by rats" was one of the milder threats.

SHINING OPPORTUNITIES

Because of Lord Henry's experiences on the western edge of the city, we tended to head the other way—toward the close-in suburbs like Forest Park and Evergreen Park. They really didn't have all that much in the way of parks. They didn't have much in the way of black folks, either. So we had to watch out. We worked the street corners and bars mostly, Thursdays through Sundays, when people were dressing up for parties and for church. We didn't have money to spare for train fare from the city to the burbs, so we'd jump the turnstiles to get on the L train. You had to time it just right, because if you jumped too early the CTA cops would bust you for not paying. It was a tough commute.

We kept our shine boxes stashed behind the trash Dumpster at a McDonald's near the L station in Forest Park. I wouldn't doubt that you'd find them still there today. We made the boxes out of wooden Pepsi or Coke bottle crates. My brothers taught me how to turn the crates over and knock out two panels with a hammer so there'd be a place for our customers to put their feet and still be storage compartments for the polish and rags. Their brotherly assistance didn't extend to sharing customers. I wasn't supposed to work their best spots or their regulars. When I first started out, it seemed like everyone I shined for turned out to be a regular customer of at least one of my brothers. They'd yell at me for horning in and then demand the money I'd been paid. Of course, they would take my money and use it to shoot dice, but they wouldn't let me in the game. I soon learned not to give up the cash easily.

My brothers had a tendency to claim everyone with feet as *their* personal clients. Hustlers hustle each other too. I got even for their tricking me by sneaking out early in the morning and going to their favorite and most profitable places, the Set Back North and Old Town West taverns. I'd get in there and shine all the shoes and get out before my brothers rolled out of bed. *Shine your shoes, sir? How much? Oh, sir, I'll accept what you give me. Will that be a spit shine or regular, sir?*

On a good day, I'd make ten dollars. If I made that much I had a "knot" to flash, but I had to be careful where I flashed it or I'd never make it home. I didn't have to worry about losing it in the suburbs. The kids there would beat me up if they could catch me, but they'd never take my money. I could never figure that out. They'd go to all the trouble of beating a guy up without robbing him. I was used to getting beaten up AND robbed in my own neighborhood. The suburban kids would give me a whipping and walk away thinking they'd got me good, while I'd be thinking, *You guys are really stupid.* Given a choice between having my butt whipped or being robbed, I'd take the butt whipping any day. (I'd like it noted that I've changed my thinking on that now that I'm older, so I hope no one gets any ideas.)

WHEN YOU COME FROM NOTHING, YOU TAKE NOTHING FOR GRANTED

Many fortunate people grow up assuming they'll get into college, earn a degree, and then get a job that'll pay them a good living. I didn't have the luxury of that assumption, and neither did anyone I knew. I'm not whining about it. In fact, I'm grateful for it. Because I wasn't handed anything, I developed keen instincts for hunting opportunities. I also have a deep apprecia- tion for those that come my way, as well as an abiding interest in helping others gain access to them. My parents stressed educa- tion above all else because they understood that the key to ele- vating your life is to prepare yourself for the opportunities that arise. The problem for many of the people I grew up with, including my brothers and many of our closest friends, is that the daily fight for survival in the ghetto distracts you from other goals. Basketball, and the guidance I got from older family members, coaches, and others, helped me stay on track. It opened a world of opportunities to me, and for that I will always be grateful.

For a long time, I'd planned on going into law and probably politics after basketball. But it gradually dawned on me that I could have a more direct impact and create more jobs for other people as a businessman. You'd only have to look at the long lists of businesses and investments that I've been involved in to see that I'm not one to pass up opportunities. I'm not impulsive about them. I consult with experienced business and investment professionals before committing my time, energy, or money. Yet, you could probably describe me as an "opportunity junkie." I look for those that will create even more entrepreneurial options so that one business breeds another, creating more jobs and widening the circle. I feel that if I'm not looking for new oppor- tunities at all times, then I'm not doing enough. For me, it's a way to keep my dreams alive.

Preparing yourself for opportunity is fundamentally impor- tant, not only because you will be ready to capitalize on those that present themselves, but also because it opens the way for you to create your own opportunities. I encourage you to read the biographies of men and women who have accomplished great things and built lasting wealth. I guarantee that you'll find many examples of them seizing opportunities that someone else missed and turning them into gold. A great source of inspiration on this topic can be found at the Web site www.horatioalger. com. If you have access to the Internet at home, at school, or at your local library, I recommend you check it out. The site belongs to a great organization called the Horatio Alger Society, which is an honorary club of sorts for this country's great opportunists. Most of the people who've been asked to join grew up with very little, yet they built lives of incredible value— not just wealth, but spiritual and social value too.

The membership list, which is available on the Web site, includes familiar names like Thurgood Marshall, Oprah Winfrey, Maya Angelou, Henry "Hank" Aaron, Quincy Jones, and Wally "Famous" Amos, but it also includes people such as:

• Dr. Dorothy L. Brown of Nashville, Tennessee, a ghetto orphan who became only the third black woman to be admitted to the American Council of Surgeons.

• *Ebony* and *Jet* publisher John H. Johnson of Chicago, whose widowed mother saved for two years so she could move her family to Chicago, because blacks were not allowed to go beyond eighth grade in Arkansas.

• Former U.S. Secretary of the Treasury Azie Taylor Morton, who grew up on a small farm in tiny Dale, Texas.

• Construction company owner Herman J. Russell, who grew up in a poor Atlanta family but built a business with annual sales of more than $280 million.

None of these people were handed opportunities, yet they prepared themselves, hunted them down, and built lives of great value by creating opportunities for others along the way. They didn't wait for Lady Luck to come knocking. They didn't put their hopes in the lottery or the blackjack table. They realized that the greatest creator of opportunities is a clear mind and a courageous spirit. I draw inspiration from the stories of the ranks of the Horatio Alger Society. I only wish that I'd known about these stories as a boy so that I could have shared them with friends and neighbors whose vision was limited by what they saw around them. Sadly, they never learned to see the opportunities ahead.

OPPORTUNITIES LOST

Dionne was one of my best friends growing up. We went through grade school together and we did a lot of hanging out. We'd tell our mothers we were spending the night at each other's houses and then stay out all night. We'd play basketball at the Boys Club until it closed around ten-thirty, and then walk the streets of the West Side like wide-eyed tourists at Mardi Gras. It was a crazy thing to do considering that the fireworks were often deadly at our neighborhood's nightly carnival. We risked all kinds of trouble from muggers, gang members, and the occasional mean-tempered cop. Even the most familiar streets were transformed in the dark. No more little old ladies and stooping old men waiting for the bus. No more kids carrying schoolbooks. Pimps and prostitutes and drug dealers ruled at that hour. Their eager, wary clientele rolled in from the city and suburbs, conducting business through open windows in high-end wheels of the sort rarely seen on our streets in daylight. It was a live-action movie filmed in darkness. Danger. Drama. Police chases. Muffled cries. We were transfixed by it all, but at that point, we were nonparticipants, "shorties," kids on a voyeuristic night out. Later, some of us would become players in the late, late show.

I had just announced my intentions to leave Indiana University and turn pro when I heard that Dionne was dead. They found him shot twelve times in the head and stuffed in a garbage Dumpster just outside the back door of his house. By that time, he was known around the neighborhood as "C-Note" because, the story went, he'd kill anybody for a hundred-dollar bill. Dionne had grown into a West Side terror. He was six-foot-two with huge biceps. He radiated raw menace. He was terrorizing the neighborhood. He was freebasing cocaine, and the only thing he could think of was getting more of it. He was hooked up with a gang, but he'd become a lone wolf. Instead of preying on people in the suburbs, he'd turned to robbing people in his own backyard. Lord Henry tried to tell him that he was headed for trouble. "I hated to see him coming, because he had death on him," my brother said.

Dionne had become the neighborhood terror because of drugs. But he was still my friend. No, it was more than a friendship. There's something about the place where I grew up that creates deeper bonds than that. I'd say it's a lot like the bonds that grow between soldiers in combat together. I would have died for Dionne and I'm sure he would have done it for me. His death hurt me deeply. It was mostly because of those deep bonds forged when we were shorties breaking curfew, but part of it was that he died just as opportunities were opening up for me. If he'd lived a few more weeks, I could have reached out to him. I could have given him chances that had been denied him. I'm usually open to anyone who comes to me to discuss a valid proposition. I respect people who try to make things happen in their lives. Other people work hard. Other people have valuable abilities and talents. But for so many of them, the opportunities just don't come, or they miss out on them for reasons they cannot help or understand.

WIDENING THE CIRCLE

As a boy, I always believed that I had it in me to do great things. That was my parents' doing. My fear was that I'd never get the chance to prove myself. From childhood my parents and others drummed into me the importance of making the most of the opportunities I was given. It began with my schooling. I watched my mother work herself to the point of collapse in order to keep us in private schools. I'll never forget her dedication. And she'll probably never forget that I kept getting booted out of the expensive Catholic schools that she worked so hard to get me into. I started out at Our Lady of Sorrows and got kicked out of there for fighting. Then I went to St. Catherine's. Fought there. Kicked out again. Finally, I ended up at Resurrection Academy. If I'd been thrown out of there, she probably would have had to change religions. My mother did whatever it took to keep us in private schools. She was outspoken and tough and she knew how to go about getting what she wanted. She'd scrub floors and do laundry for the priests and nuns in exchange for our tuition. She'd work three jobs and sometimes four. She could do hard labor, no doubt about it, but she was smart too. She ended up as a social worker for the city of Chicago, though she had no formal education in the field. She did know the territory.

When doors opened, she wanted us to see them and run through them. She believed in the ancient Senegalese proverb that says, "The opportunity that God sends doesn't wake up the sleeping."

SELF-DEVELOPMENT, PREPARATION, CONCENTRATION, AND EXECUTION

Later, I was exposed to more ancient proverbs from the chief of the Hoosier tribe, Bobby Knight. One of his many favorite sayings held that "luck is when preparation meets opportunity." Knight was a master at preparing his players for opportunities that opened up in basketball games. Self-development. Preparation. Concentration. Execution. He pounded that mantra into us so that when situations developed in the heat of a game, we responded instinctively. If we had to think, it was too late. You can't take advantage of opportunities that you can't see. You have to put in 90 percent of the work *before* the window opens. Knight's coaching techniques prepared me for a business career as much as for a basketball career. And I'm not the only one of his former players to realize that. Another is Demetrius "Tony" Brown, my roommate and teammate at Indiana University, and a guy with a history very similar to mine. Tony grew up on the South Side of Chicago, near Oakwood and Cottage Grove, which was every bit as tough as my neighborhood. Like me, he was the youngest in his family, but he had eleven brothers and sisters. Also like me, Tony went to a predominately white, Catholic school, but he played for De LaSalle Institute.

Bobby Knight recruited him and gave him a four-year scholarship to Indiana too. Given the similarities in our backgrounds, it seemed like fate that we ended up rooming together and becoming lifelong friends. We both loved basketball on several levels, but neither one of us saw the NBA as our ultimate goal. In our dorm room and at the training table, he and I talked mostly about what our lives would be like after basketball. Tony played on the NCAA championship team with me, and he left college early after being drafted by the Indiana Pacers, but he ended up accepting an offer to play professionally in Italy. He thought there might be greater opportunities for him if he experienced more of the world. And he was right.

Tony is a smart guy, always hungry for knowledge. While playing ball in Europe, he made a point of learning all he could about international business. He studied banking, commerce, marketing, and finance, and he went out of his way to make contacts in the international business community. One of those contacts began with a chance meeting in the lobby of an Italian hotel. Tony was waiting for the team bus when he struck up a conversation with an older Swiss gentleman, who told him he was a financier. The man said he worked to develop businesses in countries that most big banks avoided because they were either too small or too unstable politically or economically. "But," the Swiss financier noted, "the greater the risk, the greater the rewards."

Tony gave up his basketball career a few months later. He called to tell me that although we'd dreamed of playing together in the NBA, he had a business opportunity that he couldn't pass up. The man Tony had met was a partner with an international investment bank. With his assistance, Tony started his own financial commodity sales business. He later became CEO and majority owner of an Italian metals manufacturer's U.S. trading division. Then, within a year of becoming its chief executive, Tony bought the entire company. His company, Fuci Metals USA, based in suburban Chicago, had sales of more than $200 million a year and did business around the world. His latest venture is Commodities Management Exchange, an e-commerce metals exchange. Tony never made it to the NBA, but he does have a house next door to Michael Jordan's in Highland Park and we have vacation homes near each other on the beach. And the last time I talked to him, he was *still* looking for new opportunities. Like me, Tony has always been driven to succeed beyond the expectations others might have had for him. He was a gifted athlete, but his drive to improve his game carried him further than he might have gone otherwise. The same drive has served him well in business.

I certainly wouldn't have been able to play for Bobby Knight, or in the NBA, if I hadn't worked hard at preparing myself. Too often, kids think that the pros are all just superior athletes who play at their sports. It's not that way. When you reach that level, everyone is an athlete, but only the guys who are willing to work and adapt their games to their teammates reach the top. Another thing Coach Knight taught Tony and me is that winning is not fun. Sure, it's great to be the winner, and it's exciting to be in a game when you are winning, but the process of winning begins in practice and conditioning, neither of which are much fun. Every great player I know devotes hours and hours to practice. I knew this instinctively as a kid. There was a track and workout gym above the high school basketball court where my brothers played. I'd watch their games from up there and when one of them would make a particularly good move, I'd get up and go to a pull-up bar that was my imaginary hoop. I'd roll up a sock for a ball, and reenact what I'd seen my brother do on the real basketball court. Later, my brothers couldn't wait for me to get home from my own games so they could take me outside to a court, or to a hanger bent into a hoop and hung on a closet door, and show me what I'd done wrong in the game. I loved it because it was one of the few things I did that seemed to carry the promise of a better future. Because of all the practice and preparation I put in, I was ready for basketball opportunities when they came, just as I was prepared for business opportunities that have come since.

RACE MATTERS

Growing up in poverty gave me a deep hunger for opportunity. I was always taught that opportunities are treasures. My parents felt that way because they were denied so many chances in life because of their race and their economic status. Equal opportunity did not exist for them then, and, in truth, there is no such thing as equal opportunity today, either. I could dig out the statistics to make the point, but there's no need. I lived it every day and so do millions of other people. I was putting together a business deal recently when I learned that someone involved might be trying to thwart the deal. It could have been that the person was simply playing the game, trying to throw me off a little in order to get a better deal. That's entirely possible. It's not uncommon for such gamesmanship to go on in business deals, just like it occurs on the basketball court. Maybe it is just hard-nose business, but there is always a possibility that it's a racial thing. I don't like having to think about that but it's always there. I was talking to another West Side native a while back and he noted that when he left the city to attend college in a smaller, Midwestern town, he had trouble shaking habits from the old environment. "I was always checking to make sure no one was coming up behind me when I walked around campus at night. I was edgy, always keyed up. It was the way I'd always lived but I didn't notice it until I got out of that environment. I couldn't shake the old ways," he said.

That's the way it is with racism. It is always a potential threat to opportunity for black people. When you run into opposition, you never know for certain whether someone objects to you as an individual or because of some perceived racial threat. One of the most prominent African-American businessmen in the country was encouraged by his white business friends to join what had traditionally been an all-male, all-white country club on the East Coast. He was assured that his application would be approved because the club's white members wanted to break the racial barrier. But when the membership board was interviewing him, he had to answer this question: "If you were allowed to join our club, would you make an effort to bring in other African-Americans as members?"

His answer was, "Of course."

His application was denied.

Opportunities are particularly important to me because that same mentality is pervasive in business today. There are those who regularly deny opportunities to blacks, Hispanics, Asians, Native Americans, women, Catholics, Jews, or anyone else who didn't fit the right profile. That's not the worst of it, of course. Not too long ago, a former college basketball coach was gunned down while he was walking with his children near his home on a summer night in a Chicago suburb. Ricky Byrdsong, a good man with a wife and two children, was shot to death by a racist who was hunting down blacks, Jews, and Asians. Byrdsong was killed because he was black, and for no other reason. An even greater danger lies within the very system of justice that is supposed to protect us. A 2000 report by the U.S. Department of Justice titled "And Justice for Some" found that minority youths are more likely than their white counterparts to be arrested, jailed, sent to trial, convicted, and given long-term prison sentences. The *New York Times* noted that the racial disparities inside the justice system "are stunning. . . . Among young people who have not been sent to a juvenile prison before, blacks are more than six times as likely as whites to be sentenced by juvenile courts to prison. For those young people charged with a violent crime who have not been in juvenile prison previously, black teenagers are nine times more likely than whites to be sentenced to juvenile prison. For those charged with drug offenses, black youths are forty-eight times more likely than whites to be sentenced to juvenile prison," the *Times* reported.

White people who can't understand why blacks still feel threatened and discriminated against might want to keep that in mind, or walk in our shoes for a day or two. I don't know of a single black person who hasn't been subjected to some sort of racial profiling in recent years. When I was a vice president and general manager with the Toronto NBA franchise, I commuted from my home in suburban Detroit. Late one night, I was driving home after a game in Toronto with my assistant, Jessica, who is white. It had been a long drive, but we were just a few blocks from my office when I pulled my Explorer into a gas station. Suddenly, five police cars pulled in and I found myself staring at a bunch of cops pointing their guns at us. Jessica went into a panic. The suburban Detroit cops didn't recognize me inside the truck, so I slowly eased out with my hands in the air, and the biggest "Hi, it's me, Isiah!" smile that I could muster.

"What's the problem, officers?" I asked.

At that point, they recognized me and holstered their guns. They told me that they'd had a phone call from someone who had seen my truck swerving all over the road. They asked me to take a Breathalyzer test. I told them I'd be glad to. There was not a trace of alcohol on my breath, so the officer said, "Have a nice night, Isiah," and drove off. Now, maybe the story they told me was true. Maybe someone did claim to see my truck swerving all over the road. Or maybe a cop saw a black man with a white woman and wanted to harass them. The problem is that as a black man, I'm always faced with that question, "Why did they *really* stop me?" Like my friend from the old neighborhood, I can never stop looking over my shoulder.

I also have to wonder what might have happened that night if I had not been a black man whom the officers quickly recognized as nonthreatening. Every black person I know, rich or poor, has a similar story. My brother-in-law, a lawyer in Los Angeles, had his jaw broken by a policeman during a traffic stop there. My young nephew was arrested as he sat outside a store one morning because he fit the description of a suspected burglar. He was at the store to apply for a job so that he could help pay for his college tuition.

IN SEARCH OF A LEVEL PLAYING FIELD

Racial profiling is the worst nightmare of black mothers and fathers. It is part of the struggle we face. It's one of the reasons that our opportunities are so limited in this country. Some criticize the fact that so many young black men dream of making it in professional sports. They say that the odds against making it are extremely high, so young people should have more practical goals. Practical for whom? I agree that young people should prepare themselves for life outside of sports by working hard in school and developing their minds, but I understand why so many blacks are attracted to sports. Talent and skill rules there. The only color that matters is the color of your uniform. The scoreboard doesn't discriminate. Stat sheets aren't color coded. It's me against you, and if you can score twenty-five points a game, I want you to be on my team whether you are white, black, green, or checkerboarded.

It's not like that in the rest of the world. The playing field isn't level in most other places. Entertainment has been another traditional refuge for minorities of all kinds, yet, as you can see on television and in the movies, blacks don't often get the starring role, if they get any role at all. You'd never know from watching television that more than 12 percent of the people in this country are African-Americans. I don't know of a black man or woman anywhere who wants an advantage. Most want only a chance to compete head-to-head, fair and square. Let us have the same quality of education, the same access to health care, the same support from our local bankers, and we'll gladly take our best shot without any special help. Race is always a factor in whatever it is we try to do. Congress can pass laws, but it can't alter human nature.

Like my mother always said, "Get over it, and deal with it because that's how it is." I've had to make my own opportunities in life, and I'm glad of that because it made me strong. I don't expect anything to be handed to me. I know that I'll often have to work twice as hard and be twice as good in order to get the sort of opportunities that come easily to certain others. But I'm willing to do that if the rewards are great enough, and so far, they have been extraordinary.

A FAMILY PLAN

As a kid, I only wanted a chance to create a better life. When my basketball skills and my hard work in school began creating those opportunities, I was determined not to blow them. It's still a part of me. That hunger will never go away or be satisfied. I sometimes get the feeling that if I quit striving, I'll stop breathing. Maybe that type of hunger is the poor kid's curse, but more likely it's a blessing. I don't take opportunities for granted. If someone comes to me with an idea or a business plan, even just a thought, I hear them out. I was still with the Pistons when I became involved in American Speedy Printing and other ventures in business and real estate that have provided me with a substantial financial foundation. I had a picture of Muhammad Ali on my bedroom wall as a kid. Whether you agree with him or not, he is a man, and he has led an incredible life by standing up for what he believes in. He taught me a valuable lesson when he said that one of the worst things anyone could ever say about him after he died was that he was "just a boxer." I feel the same way. If I'm dead and gone and all they can say is that "he was a good basketball player," then I blew it.

From the day I turned pro, I was determined not to be one of those guys who walked off the court at the end of his career and had to ask, "Now what?" Basketball has meant a lot to me, on many levels, but it was never the *be-all* and *end-all* for me. I want to use life up, to make the most of every opportunity that passes within my reach. One of the few regrets I have is that I blew the opportunity to move directly from playing for the Detroit Pistons to being an executive in the organization. I had declared myself a Piston for life, and I meant it. I'd always respected those players who stayed with one team and helped create a dynasty, and I wanted to continue my relationship with the Pistons' organization and the city of Detroit. We had a great thing going there. The owner, Bill Davidson, had been a mentor to me. He'd welcomed me into his inner circle and helped give me a better understanding of how high-level business is conducted. If I'd stayed with the Pistons, it would have been a perfect segue, but we dropped the ball. We let things that didn't really matter in the long run get in the way. The deal we'd worked so hard to put together just came unraveled. And I deeply regret letting that opportunity slip away. We had our shot at it, and we all blew it.

Later, Larry Bird and Michael Jordan both left the organizations they'd played for and established themselves as coaches and executives with other teams. Magic Johnson and Joe Dumars managed to stay with their respective organizations and do well with them, so I'm hopeful that more teams will begin to value their players for their intellectual depth as much as their physical skills. Many athletes have a lot to contribute as sports and business executives. They are capable of seeing the organization from many angles.

I did learn from the disappointing experience with the Pistons, and I've certainly tried to make the most of similar opportunities that have come my way since. That missed opportunity in Detroit made me reflect on what was important in my life and how I was going to conduct myself for the rest of it. Living day to day as a boy, watching my mother and other family members struggle and suffer, I dreamed of the lifestyle that I now have. It's not just the money. The recognition that came through basketball has opened so many doors for me. It has also given me other wonderful gifts. I can walk into a room and make young people happy just by being myself. I can give encouragement and guidance. I can share pieces of my life with cab drivers, waiters and waitresses, store clerks, and other strangers who remember moments in my career as vividly, and sometimes more vividly, than I do. It really is incredible, particularly for someone for whom surviving childhood was not a particularly good bet.

I am not about to blow any more opportunities that come my way. I'm not about to spend the rest of my life on a beach, in a bar, or otherwise resting on my laurels. I'm going to keep building my life until all the tools are worn out and all the materials are spent. Of course, if I were tempted to just cruise through the rest of my life, my family would be all over me. I'd probably played in only two or three NBA games before my sister Ruby was on my case: *So, what are you going to do after basketball? You've got to be prepared, you know. This isn't going to last forever. One injury could end it all tomorrow.*

My family feels like they have a lot invested in me, and they aren't about to let their investment go bad. Don't get me wrong, it's not a situation in which they see me as their meal ticket. It goes much deeper than that. We have a love and respect for each other that few people outside our circle can understand. My sister only wants for me what I want for myself. It was a joy to play a sport that I love at the highest levels of accomplishment. But I never wanted my life to be defined by my accomplishments on the basketball court, any more than I wanted it to be defined by the limitations of the poverty I was born into. Basketball provided me with opportunities that helped me and my family break through the invisible but very real barriers of the West Side. My athletic abilities, my competitive drive, and my dedication to hard work brought rewards in the form of money and celebrity, which brought fresh opportunities and new challenges. I refuse to let any of them pass without at least giving them consideration. I know they are far too rare to do otherwise.

FUNDAMENTAL POINTS

- Preparing yourself for opportunity is important not only so that you can capitalize on those that present themselves but also because it opens the way for you to create your own.
- The greatest creator of opportunities is a clear mind and a courageous spirit.

8.

THE BEST PRESENT

A fan stopped me one day in Chicago, shook my hand, and said, "I've got to ask you this. In that game with the Knicks in the '84 play-offs when you scored about fifty points, what were you doing with the towel over your head during the time-out? It looked like you were crying."

It was Game Five. The Knicks had Bill Cartwright, Marvin Webster, Louis Orr, Ray Williams, Trent Tucker, and Daryll Walker, along with Bernard King, who was guarding me. I don't know what lit the flame, but I got hot. I just couldn't miss. Everything felt right, and I hit a streak that was unbelievable. I scored fourteen points in one eighty-four-second stretch. Then, they called time-out and I was almost delirious with euphoria. I didn't walk back to the bench. I floated. It was one of those runs that you dream of when you're in the gym taking jump shot after jump shot. It was a great, great moment and I was so damned happy I just sat there with a towel over my head, crying during the whole time-out.

Some people describe the sensation of playing like that as being "in the zone." My brother Lord Henry used to call it "getting the feeling." It's a sensation of perfection and purity. It's as though everything else is in slow motion and you are operating at the highest sensory level. You hear everything. You smell everything. You see everything. I wish everyone could experience that at least once, whether on a basketball court, tennis court, golf course, or in the bowling alley. It's a feeling that I always tried to get in every game, every time I walked onto the court. There's nothing like it. I've experienced it as a kid on the playground; in grade school, high school, and college games; and as a pro, and I can still remember each time vividly. In March of 1989, I scored twenty-four points in the fourth quarter to beat the Philadelphia 76ers 111–106 and set a team regular-season record. It was like an out-of-body experience. I could see things happening before they happened. I knew where my teammates and my opponents were going to be before they did. I had the same sort of elation in Game Six of the 1988 NBA Finals against the Lakers. I scored twenty-five points in the third quarter—setting an NBA Finals record—and forty-three total points, in spite of an ankle sprain that hurt so bad it felt like somebody had shot an arrow through it. Unfortunately, we lost the game by one point, forcing a seventh game in the championship series, which we lost.

So, the game in the 1984 play-offs is a much sweeter memory. I told that fan in Chicago that I was crying during that time-out because I was so excited and I was having so much fun. It was a strange feeling being that happy. The only other times I can think of are maybe when I'm laughing so hard I'm crying, or when my son or daughter was born. I wouldn't compare those experiences, but THAT was a great game, not just for me but for both teams. We were playing at the highest level and I loved every minute of it. I could sense every movement on the court and in the stands. I could hear whispers from the bench and scorer's table, the slap of shoelaces, the labored breathing of my opponents and teammates. Your focus is intense in those periods. All of your training and experience seems to kick in. It's like hitting the jackpot. Everything clicks and the rewards come spilling out like a river of silver dollars. The great thing about that game was that this fan, and probably many more, got into it too. They understood what was going on and they enjoyed it as much, if not more, than the guys on the floor. It was certainly a time that I will never forget, and apparently some fans have remembered it too.

ENJOYING LIFE'S GIFTS

Everyone has those joyful moments in life. They stand out in our memories because of the emotions that they stir. Exhilaration, laughter, joy; all of those elevated feelings pump up your production of endorphins, the body's natural painkillers that improve respiration, enhance our immune system, relax our muscles, and relieve stress. You gotta like those endorphins. There are ways to elevate your spirit in quiet moments too. You can take joy in something as simple as a bowl of fruit or a single grape. My wife likes to tell a story about watching me discover grapes. *That* was a moment of pure bliss for me but it was a moment of some concern for Lynn. She was probably wondering how the heck a guy could make it all the way to college without ever tasting a grape. It's true. Up to that point, I'd seen grapes on television, but I'd never tasted one. On the rare occasions when my mother had grocery money, you can believe she wasn't spending it on grapes. They were not high on her list of survival food. Do you remember when everyone got all uptight about the millennium bug and started storing up basic survival foods like water and bread and salted crackers? That was Dear's regular shopping list! So, when I saw grapes in a big fruit basket that had been given to Lynn's parents, I popped one in my mouth. I'd never tasted anything so wonderful in my life. Lynn claims that I carried that fruit basket around the house the rest of the day, slowly eating grapes one by one, savoring each bite. She's probably telling the truth. I don't remember. I was so enraptured that I lost all memory. I had fruit-induced euphoria.

Talk about your simple pleasures. There's not one much simpler than eating a grape. Yet, it was a moment I'll never forget. It was a taste I had never experienced. A luxury I'd never had. When the opportunity came to enjoy it, I really, really enjoyed it. As far as food moments go, it definitely topped my first taste of prime rib. (We are establishing a pattern here. No wonder women say the way to a man's heart is through his stomach.) I had not tasted prime rib before my high school years, when Mr. Pingatore's sister, Sandy Kasprzak, who worked in our school cafeteria, offered me a piece from her own sack lunch. She saw that I was hungry, so she said, "I've got some prime rib you can have." The only rib I'd been familiar with up to that point was *barbecued* rib. So I thought she was offering me some *prime* barbecued rib. When Sandy pulled out this sickly-looking slab of red meat, I almost lost it right there in the cafeteria.

"I'm not eating THAT!" I told her. "It's not cooked all the way and there's no barbecue sauce on it!"

She thought I was crazy. "You tell me you are hungry and you pass up prime rib?"

"That's no rib, and it sure doesn't look prime to me, it looks raw!"

It was just another case of a guy missing a great moment in life because I didn't know what I didn't know.

BASKING IN OUR MOMENTS IN THE SUN,
AND IN THE SHADE

I've read a lot of books meant to inspire and motivate the reader and often it has seemed like something was missing. That's why I've written this chapter. It is great to dream of a better life, set goals, commit yourself to achievement, and go after the life you want. Just don't forget to enjoy yourself. Don't fail to savor the great moments and the wonderful gifts that come with the journey. I've often said that I retired too early from the NBA. I blew out my Achilles tendon in the final home game in 1994. We had a lousy record that year, 20–62, even though I played in my twelfth all-star game. The Piston organization was looking to rebuild and they had talked with the New York Knicks about trading me for a number-one draft pick. I had always thought that I would spend my entire career with the Pistons. I just couldn't see myself wearing another team's uniform and moving my family to another town. I made my decision to retire based on my emotional state at the time. I wish I'd given it more thought. I wish I'd talked with some of the great players like Dave Bing and Julius Erving to see how they felt about retiring at that age. I think I had more basketball in me than I realized at that point, and since then I've thought that it wouldn't have been so bad to win a championship or two for New York and then hang up the sneakers. As it was, I retired as the Pistons' all-time leader in points, assists, steals, and games played. So, I didn't have anything to prove. But what I realize now is that I still could have had some great moments on the court. Sometimes when you look at the big picture, you don't appreciate the smaller elements. A great Chicago architect, Mies van der Rohe, said, "The beauty is in the details." It's true in architecture and in living. You don't need to have a fifty-point scoring spree to experience an enjoyable and memorable moment in life. You don't need to bungee jump into the Grand Canyon. You can take pleasure in things as simple as a grape, a sunset over the ocean, your child's laughter, your wife's grace, or even the crisp echo of a ball bouncing on a hardwood floor.

At the risk of sounding like Phil Jackson, there is something to be said in not getting so caught up in the messy details of living that you miss out on the beauty of the whole package. You don't have to be a Zen master to recognize that life is a gift and that there is reason to celebrate *every* minute we're given on this planet. One of my favorite quotes from Muhammad Ali reflects his philosophy on enjoying life: "We have stopped under this tree of life for a short while," he said. "We have stopped under a tree of temporary comfort. We have enjoyed its shade."

I try to remember that life is short so that I enjoy my moments in the sun, and those in the shade too; every year, month, day, hour, minute, and second. Like him, I want to use life up. I've come to understand that the best *present* we can ever receive is *the* present—the present moment at any given time in our lives. The clock is always ticking. There are no time-outs. So, don't wait for the right moment. Make the most of every second, it may be the only time you'll get. The perfect time is now. Enjoy it and make the absolute most of it.

MEDITATION ON THE HARD WOOD

I'm not any different from most people in that I can get caught up in what someone has said about me or done to me. I worry and I fret. I get angry, frustrated, and stressed out. I'll get all worked up and start plotting strategy about how to get even without even thinking whether it really matters. When you do that too often, you lose touch with something important—the people and things you care most about. It can happen to me even now. I lose my temper. I want to strike back. In my neighborhood, if you got hit, you hit back or you faced a daily beating. But I don't like living in that unsettled, angry state of mind. To get out of it, I'll go shoot baskets in my gym at home or wherever there is a court. It's my form of meditation. I don't go to the basketball court to relive my glory days. I go to re-create that sense of being *in the flow* or *in the zone*. I go to shake off the stress, to restore harmony in my life, to remind myself of what is really important, what I really want to do, and who I want to spend time with.

When you grow up as I did, it's difficult not to have some feelings of bitterness. We live in a culture that celebrates success and material things, and when you witness that from a seat well below the poverty line it breeds bitterness and a sense of victimization. Lord Henry was a drug addict for more than thirty years. During his addiction, you could not convince him that he was playing the victim's game. He thought he was playing it smart. Now, after years and years of battling addiction, he is clean and working as a drug counselor. Somehow, his mind was not fried in all those years of drug abuse. He's still a very sharp guy, and he's a great speaker on the topic of drug and alcohol abuse because he's seen it all, done it all, and survived to realize the tragedy of it. I've had him talk to the players about our power to choose how we respond to life's challenges. He told them that he's learned to find happiness and contentment without the artificial and ultimately deadening influence of drugs and danger. In fact, he now finds himself enjoying things that he once considered the drudgery of life. Here's a bit of what he has to say:

The way I see it now, I was a coward. I didn't step up to the plate to deal with life when it was throwing me curves. Rather than deal with it, I chose to take what, at that point, seemed like the easier and softer way out. In reality, it wasn't. The longer you stay in that subculture, the more it becomes your normalcy. Robbing and stealing and killing become a way of life. You accept it, and you derive fun, excitement, and adventure out of it. There is nothing simple about that way of life, though you may tell yourself that it is a simpler way to live than working nine to five and having a family. It's not. It is chaos and confusion.

Since I've left that life, I've had to learn how to find pleasure without drugs and the chaos that comes with them. I've learned to enjoy the true simplicity of getting up in the morning, going to work, coming home, and reading the newspaper. In my old world, that was considered a boring existence. I rebelled against that kind of life, only to find that it is the best way. It's fun for me now to go to the Laundromat and wash clothes. It's fun to be able to go to a movie and not worry about someone hunting you down and shooting you, or taking you away in handcuffs. It's fun being able to eat a meal without doing dope so that you can "enjoy it more," or worrying that if you eat you'll mess up the high from your dope. Most people take those simple things for granted, but I know they are gifts, because I lived in the other world a long, long time.

Lord Henry's experiences are off the chart as far as most people are concerned. He lived on the extreme edge of society for a long time. He and the rest of my family worked to shelter me from that world, but I've had to deal with negative emotions and impulses at my own level. You never really *escape* poverty because the experience never leaves you. That's a good thing in many ways, because you don't take anything for granted. It's good as long as you don't let it impoverish your spirit. I've seen success-ful athletes handle themselves extremely well with little prepara-tion for life in the spotlight and the material wealth that comes with an NBA contract. But I've also seen many who've become overwhelmed with their sudden affluence and celebrity. They throw money away, or they treat success as something that was owed them rather than something they earned and must keep earning.

TRUSTING IN HAPPINESS

Maintaining a balanced perspective throughout a lifetime is a challenge, no matter what course your life takes. As I was grow-ing up, it was often difficult to see much good in the world because of the hardships my family faced. I saw my mother struggling to support us. I saw my father and brothers, with all of their talents and ambitions and intelligence, knocked down by poverty and racism. I saw friends get murdered, raped, beaten up, and imprisoned unjustly. I saw cops abuse their power, and I saw good people suffer at their hands. There were many times as a kid when I was tempted to think that life was somebody's cruel joke. I could have become embittered quite easily. But I have many wonderful memories of good, happy times with my family and friends. Fortunately, I learned—mostly from my mother—to take every day as a gift, because every day, I saw that tomorrow was no guarantee.

My three oldest brothers lost their athletic promise to drugs and alcohol abuse. I helped two of them get clean later in life, but one did not make it. It is one of my great disappointments and sorrows that we weren't able to save him. Seeing my broth-ers struggle probably did more to keep me straight than anything else. I witnessed so much. I saw drug use turn into drug abuse and then into addiction and withdrawals. I saw every stage of it. I saw how it destroyed lives and brought death. I saw it turn proud men into staggering, bleary-eyed beggars. I saw it turn beautiful, sexy women into wasted-away bags of bones. I saw smart, funny people turned into zombies with dead eyes, unable to recognize their own mothers. I saw all of that and more. My brothers got into terrible situations because, from the moment they woke up in the morning, they had to support a habit and find a fix. I saw it start out as a thrill, and then I saw what it became. I'm haunted by many of those memories, but they also saved me from a similar fate. They didn't have D.A.R.E. programs in my day, but I wouldn't have needed them. I had a doctoral degree in the dangers of drug abuse by the age of thirteen.

When you see so many lives wasted and so much of life wasted and so many people and their talents and potential destroyed, the message becomes tattooed on your brain. You learn that nothing is promised. Not the next hour. Not the next minute. So you had better not waste a single second or a single opportunity. You'd better soak it all up and enjoy each tick of the clock. You'd better be grateful for what you've got and willing to share what you've been given.

RISING ABOVE BY REACHING OUT

My mother's courage and my experiences with basketball taught me that there was another side. I was inspired by her example to rise above the conditions around us. Basketball gave me a place to go where social class, money, and skin color did not decide how you were judged. The game became my portal to a more positive life, but it was even more than that. For a long, long time, the game was the only thing in my life that was pure and not tainted. It was something that I could truly fall in love with, knowing that it would never break my heart. It was always something I could get lost in. I could bury my pain on the court. There, I found peace of mind. Just being in a gym with the ball in my hands comforts me, and it reminds me that even with all of the unfairness, injustice, cruelty, and hardship, every minute is a gift.

There are a lot of things that made a difference in my life. My family's love and support. My wife's strength. The enthusiasm of my children. But probably the greatest thing that has ever happened to me is that I learned to trust happiness and to enjoy it when it comes. Most of the people I knew as a kid didn't trust it. They doubted that happiness really existed. They were suspicious of it. In some ways, they feared it because they figured it would never last, and that it was probably just setting them up to take another big hit. They trusted fear more. They believed that if someone could screw them, they'd take the opportunity. I understand where they got that attitude. But there is no joy in living like that. Fortunately, I reacted differently. Maybe I'm a natural optimist. I learned about joy on the court. I saw hard work rewarded. I saw that people could come together to achieve a shared goal, no matter what color they are, where they live, or their socioeconomic status. I also learned that happiness was not a sham or a precedent to despair. I came to see that whatever happens to me doesn't have to dwell within me. When you live with that kind of understanding, you lose your fear of life. I'm not afraid of losing every material thing I own, because I know I will survive. Take away my money, my home, my car. I'll get by. I can always go back to hustling on the West Side. I can always shine shoes and forage for food again. So I'm confident in my ability to survive. But you can't live merely to survive. It's far better to live with a sense of gratitude.

YOUR TIME TO GIVE BACK IS A GIFT TOO

I've learned to trust in happiness and to be thankful for the good things in my life. My family. My health. The opportunities that have come my way, and those that will come tomorrow. I've also learned to value the time that I've been allotted to make a difference in the lives of others. There's another important aspect of living in the moment: You realize that your time to give back isn't tomorrow or next week. It's now. You have to give back to people what you've received every day because you never know how long you'll be in a position to do it. And it could be that one day, you'll need *their* help.

One of our boyhood hustles was to wait for the Bulls players and visiting team members outside the Chicago Stadium after Bulls games. We'd stake out their cars and the visitor's bus and get between them and the door. When they'd come out we'd swarm them, asking for autographs, but mostly we wanted their shoes, their jerseys, and anything else we could sell for food money. I collected a lot of autographs and more than a few sneakers. Chet Walker, Bob Love, Campy Russell, they all gave me their shoes and their autographs.

I'll never forget one star player, a guy on a visiting team, who came out one winter night wearing a big fur coat and fur hat. I ran up to him and he turned me down cold. Wouldn't even look at me. Years later, after I had decided to turn pro, that guy came to my house and asked me to help him out in a business deal. I didn't tell him that he had once walked past me when I was looking for help. I listened to him politely and thanked him for coming. But we never did business. You only have so much time to do good and to help others. Then your time runs out. So, I don't believe in giving back "someday." I believe in giving back every day, at every opportunity.

I don't consider charity work or community service to be a favor that I do for someone else. It's a part of who I am because that's how my mother lived. Subconsciously, and consciously, my memories of the things she did still drive me to try and make a difference. She never asked people what they could do for her, but she was always anticipating the needs of individuals and the community around her. In her work at Our Lady of Sorrows youth center and around the West Side, she was more like the village wisewoman than a staff member. Everyone came to her for advice and help. My mother had nothing of value, other than her time, and she gave that freely. It was her most valuable resource. I've found that to be true with my foundation work too. We do support many organizations in the community financially, but my general philosophy is that I'd rather make an appearance, give a speech, or stage an event than write a check. It might be easier to throw money at a community cause or a social problem, but you can have a far greater impact by devoting your time and attention to it instead. My life has been touched by many people who invested their time and attention in me. They opened my eyes to hope and opportunity at a time in my life when those things were not easily seen. Most of them did it through their own examples.

You can believe that my mother didn't buy any of the respect she enjoyed with cold cash. It came from her honest dealings with people. She stuck up for anyone she believed was right and she gave hell to anyone she considered to be in the wrong. She cared enough to set that example when, many times, it might have been easier for her to take another route. I know she would have gone hungry rather than steal food. That's why my brothers lied to her so many times over the years. They'd come home with bags of groceries and tell her that they'd made some money shooting dice or shining shoes.

Mostly, they'd been using their five-finger discount cards at the local grocery store. If my mother had known she was eating stolen goods, she probably would have spit it out and gone hungry instead. She believed then, and now, that if you live unselfishly the rewards will come to you. She found her happiness in giving whatever she had to other people. Even today, she shuns material things for herself. I gave her a fur coat after I turned pro and she refused to wear it, saying, "I'm not a fur type of person." It took a lot of convincing to get her to move out of the West Side and into the house in the suburbs I bought for her. She was well aware of the dangers and the deprivation in her old environment, but she wasn't unhappy even when she was struggling to get by. Her spirit rose above it all and that's an attitude I'm always striving to achieve. My mother is proof that when you live for a cause greater than yourself—when you are devoted to helping others—then happiness comes to you in big and small ways, in bursts and flares that cannot be manufactured or purchased but should be savored, always. And that is a fundamental truth of life.

FUNDAMENTAL POINTS

- Life is a gift and there is reason to celebrate every minute we're given on this planet.
- The best present we can ever receive is the present moment.
- Whatever bad happens to you does not have to live in you. You can choose instead to focus on the best in each moment:
  - Trust happiness.
  - Live with a sense of gratitude.
  - Share your blessings.

AFTERWORD

Looking back over the past year, it's clear that I could not have picked a more turbulent—or fascinating—time in my life to write this book. In some ways it was great, but in others it was just plain crazy. From the point I started working on this book until just a few months before publication, I:

- Bought the entire nine-team CBA basketball league.
- Interviewed for several NBA head coaching jobs before taking the Indiana Pacers position.
- Sold one of my primary businesses, American Speedy printing.
- Was inducted into the NBA Hall of Fame.
- Experienced my first season as head coach of the Indiana Pacers, a team that had lost its entire coaching staff and three of its starting players.
- Had to watch the CBA basketball league fold because the NBA would not allow me to be involved in its management.

It would have been impossible to meet the deadline for this book if I had tried to keep up with every new twist and turn in my life over the last year. But in this final chapter, I would like to reflect on some of those events and how the fundamentals apply to them. I don't consciously think about them every time I put one of them into use but often when I reflect on something that's happened, I do see how I've instinctively gone back to one or more of them. I thought it might help you to understand them even better if I show how they applied to this roller-coaster ride I've been on over the last year.

A MAJOR LOSS IN THE MINOR LEAGUES

I've been a winner most of my life in sports and also in business but when I took a gamble with a venture that combined both of those fields—the CBA—I lost big. Sometimes you have a good idea and good plans and the best of intentions but you lose out because you can't control everything around you. The collapse of the Continental Basketball Association was my first failed business deal. I lost $10 million.

I purchased the CBA in 1999 because I saw it as a golden opportunity not just for me but for hundreds and maybe even thousands of others. Buying the CBA was to provide me with the opportunity to really make a contribution to the game I love, beyond those I made on the court as a player. I hoped then and I still hope to see the NBA build a solid minor league that develops talent for its teams. A true developmental league would be a great service to young players with dreams of playing professionally. Every year it seems like more and more of them are skipping college or leaving early to try and make it in the NBA. Often, they have awesome raw talent, but they lack essential knowledge of the game, or the maturity and self-discipline necessary for survival in a punishing eighty-game season. I left college early but I came out of a highly disciplined background. I'd grown up with tremendous temptations all around me and I'd stayed focused. I had a lot to learn when I got to the pros but I was ready for the challenge. Kobe Bryant skipped college but he was about the same age as me when he came into the league, because I started school early. Laker coach Phil Jackson and others have noted that after struggling for a couple years to become a well-rounded team player, Kobe made the adjustments necessary. He learned to listen to his coaches and to adjust his game to make his teammates better. Too many young athletes don't have the maturity to do that.

Leon Smith is just the latest example of a young man who was ready physically but not mentally for the NBA. He was drafted in the first round of the 1999 NBA draft by the Dallas Mavericks right out of Chicago's legendary King High School, where he was a star forward. He received a $1.45 million guaranteed contract, but Leon balked when the Mavericks asked him to refine his game either in the CBA or overseas. He became distraught and at one point reportedly attempted to commit suicide by swallowing more than two hundred aspirin. Then, he was arrested twice in one day in Chicago, apparently because of problems related to a breakup with a girlfriend. Leon, who by most accounts is a good—though troubled—young man, sought psychiatric care and at last report was trying to work his way back into the league. I feel for him. I had a difficult upbringing in some regards, but he had it worse. He was raised in a series of group and foster homes, so he never had the family support that was my salvation. I wanted the CBA to develop the talents of athletes like Leon.

Until the NBA formed its own developmental league, this country had only two levels of strong, consistent basketball competition: the NBA and the NCAA. There was a need for a third level, a place where young athletes earn the equivalent of an Ivy League advanced degree in basketball while also getting financial support and a more benevolent introduction into life in the real world of sports. Baseball has over two hundred minor league teams that prepare young athletes for the challenges of their game at the professional level. Hockey has more than a hundred teams that help young men ready themselves for the National Hockey League. Basketball is the number-one sport in America, but it had only a scattered, informal, developmental program outside of the NCAA. My goal for the CBA was to create a multitiered farm system in which players move up from one level to the next as their skills are developed so that eventually those with the highest level of development arrive ready to play in the NBA. I saw a need for this even when I was head of the NBA Players Association. Back then, I introduced a special life-skills training course for rookie players. It was a huge success and is still used as a way of helping young men make the transition into the pro game.

The CBA was an exciting venture because it combined so many of the things that fascinate me. It was an opportunity to bring professional sports back to the grassroots where families could afford to enjoy the game and feel closer to their home-town teams. I was excited also about broadcasting CBA games into new frontiers over the Internet and providing all sorts of additional content to bring faraway fans even closer to the game. Yet, I knew it was a big gamble going in. The league was in financial trouble when I bought it. The nine teams had lost more than $2 million combined with the previous year, even though attendance was at an all-time high.

In our first year, we managed to increase attendance and cor-porate sponsorship revenues by 10 percent and we expected to be profitable at the end of the season. I'd landed the CBA's first television contract and we'd already started to broadcast CBA games over the Internet. The momentum was building quickly. More than forty cities, including several in other countries, had contacted us about getting their own CBA teams.

I went to the top officials of the NBA and told them about how I wanted the CBA to become their "farm" league and they agreed it was a great idea. But instead of buying into my idea and my developmental league, the NBA decided to start a league of its own. I got aced out by the bigger player.

If the NBA had offered to become my partner, I would have jumped at it. But the big league wasn't interested in taking on a partner. I was disappointed when I learned that the NBA had decided to compete with the CBA rather than join forces with me. But I sincerely felt that the CBA could have made it on its own.

Then, when the NBA prohibited me from owning the CBA while coaching the Pacers, the writing was on the wall. Forced to put it into a blind trust, I could no longer manage the league. All I could do was wait for a buyer who never materialized. And the CBA died.

GOING DEEP TO DEAL WITH FAILURE

It was a very difficult thing for me to deal with. There were many untrue things written about the collapse of the CBA and my role in it. I was not allowed to defend myself because my contract with the NBA said I could not publicly discuss the business of the CBA while coaching the Pacers. For the record, my hands were tied. I lost out to a bigger player and while I am not happy about the failure, it happens in business all the time. In the last few months, two other minor leagues have folded, the IHL and the XFL.

While the sniping bothered me, I tried to handle it with class. I paid my debts and I'm ready to move on. To deal with the sense of loss and failure, I used one of the fundamentals described in earlier chapters. I went deep and I'll tell you exactly where I went. I went to a funeral. I can't tell you exactly which one. Maybe it was the family friend I found at the bottom of our stairs with the needle still stuck in his arm. Maybe it was my boyhood buddy Dion. Maybe it was Pee Wee. Maybe it was one of my own brothers. I've been to so many funerals. I saw so much death as a kid that I had to learn to put personal losses behind me quickly and to move on. Losing the CBA certainly wasn't as hurtful as losing a friend or loved one, not by any stretch of the imagination. It was a serious blow though. I'd invested a lot of my heart into the CBA and I'd brought in a lot of people I care about. Yet, I went deep to deal with that loss and move on, just as I had learned to grieve over far more serious personal losses.

If I'd really mourned all of the loved ones I lost, I might have given up on my own dreams. I probably would have just waited for death to catch up with me too. But I didn't do that, thankfully. I learned to move ahead and that's what I did when my plans to revive and expand the CBA died. I acknowledged that it hadn't worked out. I rejected bitterness. I even allowed myself to admire the way in which my competition had played the game and beaten me. I also took some time to savor the great moments I had putting the deal together, promoting the CBA around the country, and meeting so many great basketball fans in places like Yakima, Grand Rapids, Sioux City, and other communities.

It was my first loss in the business arena and it was a bad one. Business experts will tell you that even the most successful entrepreneurs experience failure. Often, they go through bankruptcy and worse as they attempt to carve out a successful business. Fortunately, I had the financial resources to handle the loss, thanks to my new job with the Indiana Pacers—and the challenges posed in my first season as a head coach didn't allow me much time to stew over the failure of the CBA.

LEADING THE PACERS

I can't think of another first-time coach who has faced a situation like the one I walked into in Indianapolis. After one of their best seasons ever, the Pacers had lost their entire coaching staff and three of their starters. I was following Larry Bird, a legendary player who had won high marks for his three years as a coach. Yet, I didn't have half the weapons that he'd had to work with.

If there was ever a time that I needed each and every one of the fundamentals, this was it. The Pacers veteran center, Rik Smits, decided to retire after twelve years in the league. Then we lost two more veteran starters. Mark Jackson went to Toronto as a free agent and was then traded to New York. Dale Davis also wanted to be traded, so he went to Portland in exchange for Jermaine O'Neal, a promising young player who had not seen much time on the court in his first four years as a pro right out of high school. We also lost Chris Mullen, who asked to be released from the final year of his contract so he could sign with the Golden State Warriors.

Besides Jermaine, twenty-one, two of our other young players—Al Harrington, twenty-one, and Jonathan Bender, nineteen—had come into the NBA straight out of high school while three others—Austin Croshere, Jeff Foster, and Tyus Edney—had no more than three years' experience as pros. Thankfully, we did have a few veterans—Reggie Miller, Sam Perkins, and Derrick McKey—who were not only great players but also outstanding mentors and role models for the younger guys.

MY DREAM TEAM

Before my first day as head coach for the Indiana Pacers, I started dreaming about what sort of team I wanted them to be. My vision for the Pacers is to put them on the cutting edge of the game. I want a team of big, strong athletes who can play any position. In fact, I want to get away from assigned positions on the court. I think that is where the sport is headed. We're moving toward a game in which teams don't run set plays for guards, forwards, and centers. Instead, I believe offenses will be much more free-flowing. I'm not talking about street ball or one-on-one play. It's a much more cerebral approach that takes into account the geometrics of the court with the players on it.

Lakers coach Phil Jackson and his assistant Tex Winter have a somewhat similar offensive philosophy, which they called the triangle. My vision of the game calls for moving away from recognizable offensive patterns because patterns are easier to defend against. Unlike most NBA teams, we developed a customized game plan for each team we played, which also makes it more difficult for teams to prepare for us by watching films or scouting us. It was a lot to ask of younger players and of a team that had not played together before, so we were bound to struggle.

MEASURING AT THE ROOT

We were basically a three-tier team and that's how I approached coaching my players. We had a thirty-five-and-older group with Reggie Miller, Derrick McKey, and Sam Perkins; a midlevel group with Austin Croshere, Jalen Rose, and Travis Best; and then we had our "high school group" with Jermaine O'Neal, Al Harrington, and Jonathan Bender. We used different coaching methods for each group because of their varied levels of experiences, but we taught an overall philosophy too.

My goal for this team—and every team I'd ever played for—was to win the championship. But even if that didn't happen, I wanted this mix of raw rookies, budding stars, and veteran players to have a deep understanding of what it takes physically and mentally for a team to win the NBA Finals. I knew it would be an up-and-down season. You can't really expect to bring together so many new teammates on October 4 and have them jell as a team before the start of the season twenty-five days later.

My goal wasn't so much to build a basketball team as it was to create a culture. I wanted the Pacers to have a well-defined identity so that the players, fans, and everyone involved understood what it would take to make this team and to play for it. Primarily, I want my team to be known for its great defense, its understanding of the game, and its "interchangeable parts."

COMMITTING TO SHARED GOALS AND EACH OTHER

One of the things that struck me early on was how challenging it can be to manage a group of multimillionaires. Imagine what it would be like for a businessman if each of his employees won the lottery but had to keep working for him to get the checks. That's what it is like to coach a professional basketball team.

It's my job to motivate these guys and their teammates and I am paid very well to do that. To get them to commit to our shared goals, I worked hard to create a vision for our team and to communicate that vision to them on a regular basis. At the start of the season, I gave each of the players a copy of the book *The Precious Present* by Spencer Johnson as a way to emphasize that I expected them to enjoy themselves and take adversity in stride as we moved through the year and toward our ultimate goal. One of the messages of Johnson's parable is that we need to think in the present in order to reach what may seem unreachable in the future. I told them that no matter what happened along the way in our first season, they had to commit to constant improvement over the long term so that we would be in the hunt for the playoffs.

LEADERSHIP FROM THE INSIDE OUT

I knew there would be a lot of frustration and aggravation as guys struggled to adapt and to adjust. Each group meeting was designed to serve as a forum for players to vent those feelings without tearing the team apart. Our veterans, particularly Reggie Miller, stepped up and offered outstanding leadership both on the court and off it. Reggie had his team yanked out from under him this year. I'm sure he was disappointed that so many guys left after making it to the NBA Finals the previous year. Some probably expected him to act out his anger and frustration this season. I'm here to tell you that he did not. Reggie Miller is a class act.

I really had not known him well until this year but I came to respect him not only as a player but as a person too. He stepped up under difficult circumstances and helped this team move ahead. Reggie is a superstar—one of the great clutch players in the league. Yet he put his ego aside this season and did whatever we asked of him to help this team get better. He also showed a remarkable amount of patience with the younger guys.

He spent hour after hour outside of our regular practices working with Al Harrington on his free throws. Al is a young player with a lot of potential and he probably won't realize for another six or seven years how extraordinary it was for an All-Star player like Reggie to reach out to a younger player like that. Reggie wasn't just a mentor and role model for his teammates, he became their biggest booster.

When we were in Philadelphia for the play-offs, the media announced its selections for the defensive and offensive player of the year awards. Reggie was furious that Jermaine O'Neal didn't get a single vote even though he was second in the league in blocked shots. Reggie went off on the media and gave a hilarious speech to the team that had everyone doubled up with laughter. But he also made the point that he believes in Jermaine and his teammates and his faith in them will elevate this team as much as anything I can do.

Reggie worked on himself too this season. He adjusted his game in an effort to make his teammates better and that is the mark of a true champion and a true leader.

BUILDING VALUES

At the beginning of next season, I will ask our players to put together a mission statement and to identify the values that they believe are important for the Indiana Pacers to succeed. I thought they needed a year of working together before they could do that. But I also tried to show them what I value as a coach. I tried to always put myself in the players' position and to never attack or criticize them personally. Because I was a successful player and two-time NBA champion, I also was very aware of not competing with them. I want them to know I put the team and its success before anything else.

During our first season together, we talked about the locker room as our foxhole. Every criticism or conflict within our team was handled in the foxhole, not in public. It was the place where we sought shelter from the rest of the world when others were taking shots at us. It was our place for building unity and trust, compassion and honesty—values that I am sure will stay with this team and its players for many seasons to come.

MAKING THE MOST OF OPPORTUNITIES

At the start of the season, there weren't many who thought the Indiana Pacers would make the play-offs. But I think we made the most of the opportunities we were given. I don't know of any other team that lost three starters, yet returned to the play-offs the following season. We finished the regular season with 41 wins and 41 losses. Then we gave Allen Iverson and the Philadelphia 76ers all they could handle for four games in the play-offs. They were the best team but we tested them. I know that's true because after the series, Iverson thanked us for making him a better player because we challenged him physically and mentally. We only won the first game but we were within a single shot of victory in each of the others.

I am very happy with the progress our team made in its first season. We wanted to be known as a tough defensive team and after the series with Philadelphia, that's how everyone was describing us. It's true that throughout the season I used seventeen different starting lineups, but eleven of those changes were due to players being injured or suspended. I really only changed the lineup six times and that is fairly typical because you try to adjust your team so it matches up well with your opponent. I think we accomplished what every team dreams of doing while rebuilding. We got our young guys a lot of playing time. We didn't burn up our veterans. And we still made the play-offs. We kept firing while reloading, and that's not easy to do.

ENJOYING THE MOMENTS

Now, we have a solid foundation to build upon. We have clearly defined defensive and offensive philosophies. From here on out it'll be a matter of becoming tougher-minded and more spiritually connected as a team. We have learned to trust each other and what to expect from each other. We also had a blast. Since the season ended, I've thought many times about some of my favorite moments and experiences in my first year as a coach. I smile whenever I think about Reggie Miller stepping up and working with the younger players after practice. I smile when I think of the incredible progress made by our younger players on the court, and off it too. There are other things. I will never forget Derrick McKey and Sam Perkins giving up their starting positions and stepping aside for younger players. They did it with class and grace. Not one day went by that they didn't try to help the players that started in their places. Both of them worked with those younger players to help them become the best they can possibly be. You hear a lot these days about athletes who care only about themselves. It was a joy to watch those veteran players do what was best for their team without complaining and, in fact, with complete selflessness.

At the start of the season, I told people that I thought I'd like coaching. By the end, I was telling anyone who'd listen that I loved it. It was a challenging year, but it sure made for an interesting and rewarding life. I think that is the best present of all, don't you? Here's wishing that yours is exactly what you want it to be.